Endorsements

"Teachers want to teach and students want to learn skills that map to twenty-first-century careers. Adobe Spark has struck a nerve because it helps build visual communication and problem-solving skills by making creation fast, fun, and frictionless. It has been so gratifying to see the impact that Spark has had in the classroom, and Monica Burns and Ben Forta have been guiding educators from Day 1. This book will let you benefit from their insights and help you get the most out of Spark, regardless of your task or curricular objective."

—*Aubrey Cattell, VP, Adobe Spark + CC Education*

"Adobe Spark is a digital creation game changer, and educators Burns and Forta have created the resource to empower any teacher to make students' thinking visible and their learning come alive with this simple yet powerful tool. *40 Ways to Inject Creativity into Your Classroom with Adobe Spark* is a clear and practical guide to take student communication, reflection, and creation to the next level. Burns and Forta don't give us a 'how to use Adobe Spark.' Instead, they focus on 'how to make student creation the driver of learning.' This book is standards driven, keeping the focus on the learning and not on the tool."

—*Rebecca Hare, art and design educator and author of* The Space: A Guide for Educators

"This comprehensive collection of innovative Adobe Spark projects is a creative shot in the arm for anyone seeking to diversify the digital learning artifacts produced in their classrooms. Ben and Monica provide proper insight and inspiration to get learners of all ages creating and communicating with original media content. Their detailed lessons are easy to follow and ready to use tomorrow."

—*Andy Leiser, elementary integration specialist, Hastings, Minnesota*

"I have admired the work of both Monica and Ben for years. In this book, they have created an incredible compilation of the creative power of Adobe Spark tools that will allow readers to start integrating technology in a powerful way, right away! Each lesson gives teachers the capacity to offer their students (and themselves!) a chance to creatively express their knowledge and ideas. The projects infuse technology in a way that promotes student voice and choice and allows their learning to be presented in creative and meaningful ways. The emphasis on reflection, collaboration, and strong visual communication skills makes this book a true gem in an edtech space that is many times focused on digitizing worksheets or simple updates to analog practice."

—*Michael Cohen, The Tech Rabbi and author of* Educated by Design

40 Ways to Inject Creativity into Your Classroom with Adobe Spark Sp

Ben Forta & Monica Burns

40 Ways to Inject Creativity into Your Classroom with Adobe Spark

Published by EdTechTeam Press

Library of Congress Control Number: 2018957491
Paperback ISBN: 978-1-945167-51-5
eBook ISBN: 978-1-945167-52-2

Irvine, California

Contents

Creativity is as important now in education as literacy,
and we should treat it with the same status.
—*Sir Ken Robinson*

All students have stories to tell. Be it about their learning, their families, their experiences, their ambitions, or their daydreams, children love to tell stories; they are naturals at it! But storytelling isn't just fun and games. Storytelling is fundamental to both creativity and communication, which is why innovative educators constantly seek new ways to inject storytelling into their classrooms.

Students today have the ability to consume a world of content as viewers, readers, and listeners on their digital devices, but content consumption isn't enough if they are going to master those essential skills of creativity and communication. As educators, we must help our students shift from being content consumers to content creators, and that means providing opportunities for students to tell the story of their learning and share their new knowledge with the world. From persuasive videos designed to convince an audience to take action to websites that capture the steps in a science experiment, students of all ages can share and celebrate their learning with digital tools—and with Adobe Spark, it's easier than ever.

Adobe Spark is a free and simple-to-use creation tool that empowers students of all ages to tell their stories. Designed to be fun, approachable, and accessible, Spark works on just about any of the devices in your classroom. It runs in the web browser on all computers and has been optimized to run on Chromebooks. In addition, Spark is available as a series of mobile apps for iOS (for iPads and iPhones).

As educators who believe in the power of technology used with purpose and intention, we have embraced the Adobe Spark creation tools. Monica Burns is a former New York City classroom teacher always on the hunt for free tools to use in her one-to-one iPad classroom. When she first came across the Spark tools, she knew they would be a game changer for students and educators. In Monica's role as an education consultant, speaker, and blogger, she has shared Spark and ways to infuse creativity into every subject area—at all grade levels. Ben Forta comes from a family of educators, and has been teaching for more than three decades. His books, many of which are used as college textbooks, have taught coding to more than a million people. He currently helps drive Adobe's education agenda, focusing on ways to improve creative and digital literacy in classrooms the world over, and he has played a key role in evolving Adobe Spark into the powerful edtech tool it has become.

Your students are natural storytellers and, armed with the right tools, their creativity will flourish. Our goal with this book is to equip you with the know-how and a wealth of ideas for helping your students stretch their creative muscles.

> Explore Adobe Education's research paper, "Creative Problem Solving in Schools: Essential Skills Today's Students Need for Jobs in Tomorrow's Age of Automation": cps.adobeeducate.com.

 **for Education**

Your first port of call for all things related to Spark in the classroom should be the Spark Education page at spark.adobe.com/edu. With the mission of ensuring that educators have the tools they need, Adobe offers Adobe Spark for Education. The key features of this program are critical for schools and helpful for our students. These include better data privacy, easier logins, restricted public image search, sharing restrictions, and more control for educators. Enhanced data privacy means that schools can deploy Adobe Spark for Education in a manner consistent with children's data privacy laws such as the Children's Online Privacy Protection Act (COPPA). Logins for students and schools can be set up with single sign-on so students can quickly log in using their existing school ID; they won't have to set up a separate Adobe ID. Schools will own the accounts and exercise admin rights over them as well. On top of all those perks, Adobe Spark for Education users get Spark's premium features for free (a savings of $9.99 month per user).

You can find Adobe's Student Privacy Policy online at
adobe.com/privacy/student-policy.html

 in the Classroom

Adobe Spark offers three ways for student storytellers to create and share: Spark Page, Spark Video, and Spark Post. These can be used independently or in conjunction:

Spark Page is a web page creation tool in which students can use text, images, videos, and links to create a story that can be viewed in any web browser.

Spark Video is a moviemaking tool students can use to bring icons, images, videos, text, and music together with voice narration to create a movie.

Spark Post is a graphic design tool in which students can layer text over one or more images and color blocks to create a graphic in any size.

Teachers love Spark because it imposes no "right way" for students to create. Students can create a Spark Post to spotlight a quotation from a book they are reading. They could use Spark Video to document the steps for solving a math problem or to reinvent book reports. Or Spark Page might be the tool to reflect on the outcome of a science experiment. As you'll see in this book, the possibilities are endless!

How to Use This Book

This book includes lessons, graphic organizers, and stories to help you promote creativity in your classroom, and many of these ideas were inspired by teachers like you. Each lesson contains similar components and should be viewed as a guide, not a script. Use these lessons as inspiration, taking into account the unique needs and interests of your students.

Here are a few words we use throughout the book:

- Exemplar: example of a final project that showcases all of the elements you would like to see in a student product

- Think aloud: moments in which you share your thought process or decision-making process with students so they can watch as you problem solve

- Media: any type of images, icons, or video content

- Domain-specific vocabulary: words related to your unit of study that you would like students to learn and apply in their work

Throughout this book you will see lessons in which the grade levels range from K–12. Of course the same lesson wouldn't be taught in both a kindergarten and a high school classroom. You can tailor each lesson to your students by varying the ways you group students, scaffold the lessons, customize expectations, and allow for choice and voice.

Some lessons and activities refer to online resources. Including URLs to resources in a printed book is never ideal, because typing long URLs is asking for trouble. You'll find all of the links in this book on the book's web page at forta.com/books/spark.

Adobe Spark is an intuitive, simple creation tool; that's why we love it! If you haven't used Spark before, the "plus sign" is your best friend. It gives you the power to add media to your Spark creations and customize your final product. You'll find extra tips for using Spark when you open the tool on your device. Because tools like Spark periodically receive updates and new features, we decided not to include any screenshots in this book. We're confident you can dive in right away and find any extra help on the website linked on this page.

Getting Started with in the Classroom

We are so excited that you are committed to turning students into creators this school year! We've seen the power of the Adobe Spark tools in schools around the world, and this is your chance to help your students shine. Promoting creativity in the classroom is essential for students of all ages. With Adobe Spark for Education, you can introduce open-ended creation tools to students and give their learning a space to shine!

Ready to deploy Adobe Spark for Education? Your school's IT Administrator can deploy Spark from their Adobe Admin Console. All of the directions for getting started can be found at: spark.adobe.com/edu.

For additional educator content, including a growing library of exemplars, student work, lesson plans, and more, visit the Adobe Spark page on the Adobe Education Exchange at: edex.adobe.com/spark.

APP SMASHING WITH

Use the interactive presentation tool Nearpod to link to Spark Video and Spark Page creations. Add the link to a video or page to your Nearpod presentation so students can view it directly on their device. Alternatively, try creating slides for Nearpod in Spark Post. You can find more tips here: classtechtips.com/2018/06/25/adobe-spark-and-nearpod.

Flipgrid is a dynamic tool for classrooms. Students can share recorded video reflections and submit work in a space shared with their peers. Ask students to share a link to their video or add a video describing their project.

You can find more tips here: classtechtips.com/2018/03/13/share-spark-video-flipgrid.

Oh, one last thing. We love discovering new ways passionate educators use Adobe Spark in the classroom. So please do share; we would love to hear from you.

Share your student and teacher creations on social media using the hashtag #SparkMade and #CreateEDU.

Ben Forta
@benforta
forta.com

Dr. Monica Burns
@classtechtips
classtechtips.com

Lessons

#1 Welcome Back Message

Welcome your class back to school with a fun video message.

Grade Level
Tailor your video to your student audience K–12

Time to Complete 🕐 40 minutes

Assistance Needed
This activity is perfect for teachers using Spark for the first time and who want to explore the tools. Use this Welcome Back Message as an exemplar for a student-created project such as a Student Introduction Video.

Instructions

Use Spark Video to create a welcome message for students and parents. Be sure to include a photo of yourself (or a video if you are feeling brave) and contact information.

Some teachers find that Spark Video is also a great way to share and explain classroom rules, expectations, and policies with students. You may find that your students are more likely to watch a video than listen to you talk.

Here is a list of items you may want to consider or include as you organize your Welcome Back Video:

- Title slide with class name/teacher name

- Reasons why you are excited for the new school year

- A few things students can expect to learn and explore in the first quarter of the year

- Expectations or class rules

- A personal story of something special you did this summer

- Your personal and professional goals for the school year

- Contact information

You can also create a Spark Page and embed your Spark Video in it. By doing this you can add clickable links to school webpages, your contact information, and more. It's a great way to organize resources for students and families.

Tips & Extensions

- Make sure to publish your video (and page) or no one will be able to see them. The Share button at the top of your screen takes you through the steps on how to publish your creation.

- If you opt to create a Spark Page with an embedded Spark Video, create the video first and publish it. You will then see a content URL that you can copy and paste into the Spark Page.

 **TEACHER STORIES**

"I used Adobe Spark with both my third and fourth graders. Both classes created Adobe Spark Videos as performance tasks to demonstrate their learning of material covered in ELA/Social Studies class. The fourth graders completed a unit on the thirteen original colonies. One of the projects to choose from was to create a video persuading future colonists to settle in the colony that they chose to research. The third graders were learning about geography and landforms. They each researched a famous landform that they wanted to learn more about, and created a video to 'show and tell' about the landform they selected. Their videos were posted on their digital portfolios and were shared with other classmates and parents. Students in both classes assessed their videos and completed a self-reflection of their learning and understanding of the big idea presented."

—Amy Nass, third and fourth grade ELA/social studies teacher, Port Republic School, New Jersey

#2 Student Introduction Videos

Students will introduce themselves to their fellow students by creating a personal welcome video. (Teachers may want to do the same to introduce themselves to their students.)

Grade Level   K–12

Educational Outcomes
To acclimate to a new class or teacher, students will create a video to introduce themselves, highlighting what they want their classmates to know about them.

Time to Complete 🕐 40 minutes
Assistance Needed
Students may need guidance on appropriate levels of sharing, finding supporting imagery, and getting started recording their own voices.

Instructions

(5 minutes)
Ask students to write down five key things they'd like their classmates to know about them. Suggest they share something about their family, where they are from (prior school if appropriate), favorite activities and foods, and places they have visited.

If you created a Welcome Back Video, you can use it as an exemplar for students.

(15 minutes)
Using Spark Video, have students create an "About Me" title slide, and then add a slide for each item they want to share. Encourage them to search for images and icons. You may want students to sketch a storyboard of the five fun facts about themselves that they would like to share with their classmates.

You may want to create a checklist for students or provide a few prompts to help get their wheels spinning. Here are a few ideas that you can tailor to your students:

• Share your favorite food.

• Describe one place you visited this summer.

• My favorite movie is…

- If I could play one video game every day for a year, it would be…

- When I think about my goals for the future, one thing I want to accomplish is…

(10 minutes)

Have students record a single narrated sentence for each slide. Show them how to play back their voice, and explain that they can rerecord as needed. If you have a large classroom and everyone is recording at once, ask students to tilt their device so the microphone is closer to their mouth. Alternatively, students who have earbuds or headphones in their backpack can use them to capture their voice.

(5 minutes)

Show students how to browse themes and music to pick one for their video. You may want to talk about the different types of music options and the words used to describe each category.

(5 minutes)

After students have created their Spark Video, ask them to share it with you. They can save it as a link or download it as a video file. Then students can share their video using Google Classroom, Flipgrid, Seesaw, or a similar platform.

Tips & Extensions

- If using Spark Video on an iPad, have your students use the device camera to take a selfie for use on the video title screen.

- Encourage students to use personal images from their own devices as appropriate. Alternatively, you could ask students to only use icons for this project; they can search for symbols related to their sentence.

#3 Daily Video Journal

The Daily Journal is a staple of many classrooms, a short creative project to start each day. Here the daily journal is reimagined as a fun and inspiring video project.

Grade Level   2–6

Educational Outcomes
Students will create a daily video recording to capture their growth related to content area goals.

Time to Complete   5 minutes per day
(after initial setup time)

Assistance Needed
After introducing this routine to students, you may want to modify prompts or instructions for students over the course of a unit of study.

Instructions

On Day 1, have each student create a Spark Video project entitled "My Daily Journal." To truly personalize the video, encourage them to use their own picture on the title page. They can choose a theme that reflects their style.

Introduce the concept of journaling to students by making a connection to a routine that may already be established in your classroom. Explain that the goal is to talk about their learning each day and add to a Spark Video creation.

Each day, students add a single slide containing an icon, image, or text to the video. Have them then record the narration for the new slide, starting with the day and date, and then the journal entry itself. Encourage students to practice what they will say before recording their entry. Their recording should be concise and to the point.

You may want to guide students through this activity by providing a prompt for them to follow. During the first week of creating a video journal, ask students to use a prompt such as "One thing I learned today..." The next week you could give students a variety of options for sentence starters, such as...

- I am still curious about…

- I think I could have done a better job at…

- I'm so proud I was able to…

As the video grows each day, students will see their own progress and proficiency in video storytelling. You could have students create one video each month or compile reflections during a two-week or six-week unit of study.

Tips & Extensions

- A single video for the whole school year may be too long. Some teachers have students create a new video each week or month; adapt this idea to best suit your classroom.

- Remind students to publish their changes. Otherwise, the published video won't include any new journal entries. When they use the Share button to republish their video, it will update the link to include the new content.

- Spark Videos have unique URLs that do not change even if a video is updated. This feature is especially helpful with a project such as this. The Video Journal link can be shared with family, for example, and each time they view the video it will have grown with new entries.

#4 Video Book Reports

Encourage reading in your classroom and gauge reading comprehension with video book reports.

Grade Level   4–8

Educational Outcomes

Students will capture special moments from their reading to spotlight literary elements from their reading.

Standards Connection

Reading Literature: comprehension and literary elements

Writing: summarizing and using textual evidence

Time to Complete   🕐 50 minutes

Assistance Needed

Students should be encouraged to plan their video book report before jumping in to create slides. Define what literary elements need to appear in their book report, including title and author, characters, location, plot, and a personal recommendation at the end.

Available on page 114.

Instructions

(10 minutes)

Students create lists of the key points needed in their video book report. You may want students to structure their video book report in a specific way. A graphic organizer can help students plan their Spark Video. If your students summarize their reading each day in a notebook, they can refer to these notes as they prepare their video book report.

Sharing an exemplar with students can help them envision their final product. If you have created a video book report or found an example, take time to share it with students.

(5 minutes)

Ask students to create a new Spark Video project. The first slide should contain only the book title and author. Have students create a slide containing the title of each report section (characters, location, etc.). You may want to provide a checklist for students to help them organize their video.

(15 minutes)

Students add slides to each section, looking for icons that support their points. Icons are preferred over photos and images, because they tend to be more abstract. This requires students to focus on their own message as opposed to describing what is in a photo. The icon library in Spark offers a wide range of choices.

(10 minutes)

Students record a single sentence for each slide. Show them how to play back their voice, and explain that they can rerecord as needed. When students are ready to record, you may encourage them to find a quiet corner of the classroom or use headphones.

(5 minutes)

After students have created their Spark Video, ask them to share the link with you. You could spotlight a new video book report to your class each day to inspire them to find a new title to read.

Tips & Extensions

- Starting a video report by posing questions is a good way to have students think about a book's key messages and themes. Examples may include "How would you feel if you moved to a new town where you knew no one?" or "Could you imagine growing up thinking you were nothing special, and then discovering that you were actually a wizard?" These prompts can be included in the story as slides after the title and before the first content section.

- Encourage students to browse Spark Video themes and music to find one that properly supports their report and connects to the theme of their book.

#5 Interesting Quotations

Students will capture quotations as they read and then create a Spark Post graphic. This graphic will combine the quoted sentence with an image or series of images.

Grade Level   2–12

Educational Outcomes
Students will attend to text (in any subject area) to cite a relevant, interesting, or thought-provoking quotation to share.

Standards Connection
Reading Information/Literature: textual evidence

Reading Information/Literature: close reading

Writing: curating digital media

Time to Complete   45 minutes

Assistance Needed
Students will need to access content-specific reading material. This could include a novel during independent reading, a current events article in the science classroom, or any type of text.

Instructions

(10 minutes)

Introduce new reading material to the class. This reading material should be specific to your grade level and/or content area. State the task for today's lesson:

Today, you will read __[novel, article, blog post, etc.]__ and choose one sentence that inspires you or you find interesting. It should be a sentence that makes you feel a certain way, provides advice, or offers wisdom.

Model for students how you can annotate a passage or jot down a few inspiring quotations as you read; for example, you could read an article from Newsela and model for students how you underline interesting sentences.

(20 minutes)

Provide time for students to read independently or with partners. As you circulate, encourage students to annotate their text or jot down a quotation in their notebook. In a social studies classroom, students might read primary source documents, such as a speech, during this activity. In a math classroom, students could read an article that discusses an innovation in space travel.

In the last few minutes of this lesson, ask students to share the quotations they collected with a small group or with a partner. Have students choose one quotation that stands out to them.

(15 minutes)

Pose the question to your class: "How can we share our reading with the world?" Ask students to share a few examples.

Bring students together to watch you take just a minute or two to create a Spark Post quotation card. Open Spark Post and choose a background image that relates to your quotation. Think aloud for students as you use more than one search term to find the perfect picture. Add your quotation to the page and include the name/source. Show students how you can modify the design before pressing the Share button.

Provide time for students to create their own quotation cards. As you circulate, you can support students as they choose a color scheme or toggle between different designs. Students can use the Share button to send their Spark Post creations to you.

Use the last few minutes of class time to allow students to walk around the classroom and read the quotations displayed on their classmates' screens.

Tips & Extensions

- If students are capturing quotations from a novel, share their Spark Post creation on Twitter, and tag the author's handle. Here is a helpful resource: classtechtips.com/childrens-authors-on-twitter.

- Reach out to the person at your school or district who manages social media. Ask them whether your students can share their Quotation Cards on a social media platform.

#6 Community Highlights

Students will show off a special event, person, or place within their school or local community. They will create a Spark Video that shares a community highlight while exploring how to present information to an audience.

Grade Level   K–12

Educational Outcomes

In a profile of their community, students will use interviews, field trips, and research to create a multimedia product.

Standards Connection

Reading Information: conducting research on a topic

Writing: text structure and organization of material

Science: content-specific goals

Time to Complete   45-minute lesson to create Video (additional time allocated for research)

Assistance Needed

Students can gather information through independent research or through teacher-directed exploration of a topic. This activity can be tailored for age; younger students can create a class video, and older students could work collaboratively or independently.

Instructions

Project Brainstorm

Bring students together and pose the question, "What are some special things about our community that we can share with the world? What special events take place here? Who in our community has a compelling story to share?" Ask students to share their thoughts with a partner.

Display three columns on an interactive display board or chart paper. Title the columns (1) Special Events, (2) People, (3) Places. Ask students to help you list several items under each section.

With a group of younger students, you may want to choose one topic for your class to explore. Then create one video as a class, with a slide for each student.

With an older group of students, consider having students choose a topic to investigate independently or in a team.

Video Planning

As students get ready to conduct their research, pose the following questions to your group. You can tailor these questions to your expectations for students.

- Where will you go to find information on this topic?

- Why is this topic significant to our community?

- Why is this worth sharing with the world?

- What should you include in a video on this topic?

As students dive into their research, consider providing an exemplar, rubric, or checklist that is specific to your goals for students.

In preparing to spotlight something special about your community, students can participate in a field trip, take a community walk, interview a local historian, or research using print or online resources.

Video Creation

After students have conducted their research, bring the group together. Ask younger students to pick one thing they think is important about the topic and decide what they will say and what type of image or icon should appear on the screen. With this type of class project, younger students can record their idea and search for media with teacher support. For older students working individually or in pairs, ask students to open Spark Video on their device. They can add a title slide with their topic followed by slides that share information to spotlight something special in the community.

Tips & Extensions

- Review the English / Language Arts goals you have for students. Even if this is a project in the science classroom, you have the opportunity to connect to ELA expectations for students, such as word choice, voice, or organization of ideas.

- Share students' videos on a community website, local event page, or through a school alumni network. Your students can brainstorm possible audiences that connect to the specific focus of their Spark Video.

#7 Math All Around You

Make math concepts, from counting to fractions, real and relatable for students. Children can present findings in a video using their voice and multimedia.

Grade Level   1–4

Educational Outcomes
Students will use math concepts and vocabulary connected to grade-level-specific goals.

Standards Connection
Math: customize for grade level

Math: domain-specific vocabulary

Speaking and Listening: describing objects

Time to Complete   35 minutes

Assistance Needed
When students capture pictures of math in action, have them use the camera on the same device they will use to access Spark Video. This will ensure a smooth workflow when students are ready to upload pictures.

Instructions

(5 minutes)
Set the stage for the activity by explaining that students will search for math all around them. You will want to customize your instructions to the grade-level-specific goals you have for students:

- Students learning numbers would need to find items with a specific count (2 doors, 3 light switches, and so on).

- Students learning fractions would need to find items that represent those fractions (4 panes of glass in the door, 4 quarters = 1 whole).

(15 minutes)
Give students a target number of objects to find based on age and complexity of task (Finding sevenths isn't easy!). You may want to model for students how you have located an example so they can watch as you think aloud and problem solve.

Students can walk around the classroom, the school, even the playground or schoolyard, looking for objects matching what they need to find. Ask students to take a picture of each object.

(10 minutes)

Armed with their pictures, students create a Spark Video with a single slide for each picture. Students should then record a description ("There are 10 pencils") or an explanation ("There are 4 windows in this door, 4 quarters = 1 whole") for each.

Students should also create a title slide introducing their project. If students are working in a small group, each student in the group can take turns sharing the different objects they have found.

(5 minutes)

After students have created their Spark Video, ask them to share it with you. They can save it as a link or download it as a video file. Then students can share their Video using Google Classroom, Flipgrid, Seesaw, or a similar platform. You may want to introduce a new workflow for students or use an online space students have used before.

Tips & Extensions

- This activity works best on devices with built-in cameras, including iPads and Chromebooks.

- This concept can be varied for learning letters (finding things that begin with the letter A), colors, shapes, and more. You could also introduce this concept of searching for objects during cross-curricular scavenger hunts.

#8 Video Storytelling

A fun modern take on creative storytelling. Students will tell their own video story, using their pictures and in their own voices.

Grade Level   K–5

Educational Outcomes
Students will tell a story in a sequence, using imagery.

Standards Connection
Storytelling: composing a narrative

English Language Arts: customize to grade-level-specific ELA standards

Time to Complete   90 minutes
Assistance Needed
This is a longer project and should be broken into three parts over multiple days: planning the story, creating the artwork, and compiling the video. You can tailor this project to ELA goals or specific state or national standards.

Instructions

(15 minutes)
Discuss stories and storytelling with the students. What stories do they like and why? What makes a story fun and engaging? What characters and locations do they like?

Share examples with students of stories you've explored as a class, such as a favorite novel or read-aloud picture book.

(10 minutes)
Help students determine what pictures their story will need. For very young students, two or three pictures will probably suffice; older students should be encouraged to break their stories into more granular pieces.

Ask students to share their stories with a partner. Students can use words that signal order or the passage of time, such as first, then, next, or finally.

(40 minutes, spread over multiple days)
Students should draw, color, or paint the pictures for their story. For the best result, each picture should be a full 8.5×11 (or A4) page with the drawing filling as much of the page as possible. You can use a range

of materials to help students create the image for each part of their story.

(5 minutes)
Students take a picture of each of their story pages. On an iPad these can be saved to the Camera Roll; on other devices they should be saved to any shared storage or folder. Students will need to access these photos to upload them to their Spark Video.

(5 minutes)
Help students create a Spark Video project. Have them create a slide for each of their story pages and then add one story page to each slide. Have them play their video to get an idea of what their final creation will look like.

(10 minutes)
Students record their story narration for each story slide. Show them how to play back their voice, and explain that they can rerecord as needed. Encourage students to practice what they will say before recording their voice.

(5 minutes)
After students have created their Spark Video, ask them to share it with you. They can save it as a link or download it as a video file. Then students can share their Video using Google Classroom, Flipgrid, Seesaw, or a similar platform.

Tips & Extensions

• Younger students tend to want to create one big picture for their story. Although this works, the final video won't be as fun to view. An alternative would be to help students take multiple photos of different parts of their story picture, using these individual photos for the story slides.

- If appropriate, ask students about the story mood. Is it happy? Exciting? Scary? Funny? Then help them find background music that matches the mood.

- Adobe Spark Video includes a library of music licensed for use in your videos. If students want to use their own music (which Spark Video supports), you'll want to have an age-appropriate discussion with them about digital citizenship and content ownership and rights.

- Students who finish the project quickly could be encouraged to create a title slide for their video story, using their own picture, a selfie, or a text title.

TEACHER STORIES

"I have used Adobe Spark three ways for different year levels. My Year 4 students made a news report about different aspects of Aboriginal culture. They imported videos of themselves that they recorded on their laptops and combined them with stills with voiceovers to create continuity. While we were exploring text structures, Year 5 students used it to create an explanatory video showing the sequential steps for performing a dance of their choice. They could use stills and captions to demonstrate the individual moves of the dance and then add video to show the combination of steps. They were also able to import the appropriate music for their dance. Year 6 students have used it to create a book trailer using mostly still images. They were able to import their book cover and other pictures from the internet and create mood and suspense using music and graphics. The students found it so easy to use."

—*Deirdre Hughes, teacher/librarian, Perth, Western Australia*

#9 Create a Haiku

Introduce students to haiku poetry to compose a poem in pairs. Using Spark Post, students can choose an image or color for the background and add the text of their haiku to create a shareable poem.

Grade Level   3–6

Educational Outcomes

After reading examples of haiku poems, students will write a haiku with a partner.

Standards Connection

Speaking and Listening: collaborating with peers

Reading Literature: exploring poetry examples

Writing: creating poems in haiku format

Time to Complete   🕐 45 minutes

Assistance Needed

Students may need support with identifying keywords when searching for images. You may want to model how to search for images using a few different keywords.

Instructions

(10 minutes)

Introduce your students to examples of haiku poems. Pose the questions, "What do you notice about these poems? What do they have in common?" Ask students to think-pair-share and discuss their observations.

Bring the class together to review these examples and share your observations aloud. You might say, "I notice that a haiku poem has three lines," and, "I notice that there is a pattern using syllables."

Establish a definition of a haiku that works with your learning goals for students. This could include introducing a new term such as syllables or lines. Model for students as you write a haiku poem, and think aloud as you count the syllables on each line. You may want to suggest a focus for the haiku poems students will write, such as a season or theme.

(15 minutes)

State the task for today's lesson: "Today you will write haiku poems with a partner and create a Spark Post to spotlight one of your poems."

As students work in pairs to write haiku poems, circulate to answer questions and encourage students to consider incorporating new vocabulary in their writing. Have them write their poems on a piece of paper, in their notebooks, or in an online space such as a collaborative Google Doc.

Encourage students to write multiple haiku poems together and choose one they would like to share with their classmates.

(15 minutes)

Introduce students to Spark Post, including how you log in and get started with your creation. Model for students as you take one of your poems and turn it into a Spark Post. You'll want students to see how you brainstorm keywords to search for a background image and choose a font and colors that connect to the mood and tone of your poem.

In this task, students are working in pairs, so one student will log in to their account. Encourage students to talk to their partner and compromise as they make decisions on font, color, images, and text placement.

When students are finished, have them download the Spark Post they have created to their device or create a link to share.

(5 minutes)

Ask students to share their haiku poems with their classmates. Project the poems students make on an interactive display screen in your classroom, or have students walk around the room to show off the Spark Post creations displayed on their individual screens.

Tips & Extensions

- If your school has an Instagram page, students can make a Spark Post shaped in a square. This will make it easy to share their haiku on this social network.

- Students can create multiple haiku poems with Spark Post and compile these images into a slideshow with Spark Video.

- Use this reference article from the Academy of American Poets for more information on Haiku poetry: http://poets.org/poetsorg/poems.

#10 Rhyme Time

Students will practice word sounds by creating a rhyming video.

Grade Level K–4

Educational Outcomes

As students explore language skills, they will record their voice to capture their learning.

Standards Connection

Language: letter sounds

Speaking and Listening: fluency

Time to Complete 30 minutes

Assistance Needed

This lesson asks students to search for icons to represent words that rhyme. You may want to lead a younger group of students through this activity as a whole group or small group. If your students will search for icons using keywords, you may want to display these words to the class, so they can spell each one correctly.

Instructions

This activity uses Spark Video's split screen layout to display rhyming icons side by side. Use the Layout button at the top corner of your screen to switch from one layout to another. Locate this button to practice switching Spark Video layouts before modelling this activity for your students.

(5 minutes)

Open Adobe Spark and create a short Spark Video yourself to show to the entire class. Switch the layout to split screen so two items can appear side by side. This activity works best with icons (rather than photos), so show students how to search for and add an icon to one side.

Example: Show students how to search for an icon showing a "mouse." Ask the students for a word that rhymes with "mouse" (it'll inevitably be "house"), and add that icon to the other side of the screen. Then record your narration "mouse rhymes with house." Then play your video for students to view the slide you created.

(20 minutes)

Now it's the students' turn. Give them a target number of rhyming words to find. For younger students, start with just two or three; older students could easily find as many as eight or ten in this time.

Depending on the level of support that the students need, you may provide a list of words for them to use.

Ask students to create a split layout slide for each pair of rhyming words, adding one icon to each side, and then recording the narration, as you did.

(5 minutes)

After students have created their Spark Video, ask them to share it with you. They can save it as a link or download it as a video file. Then students can share their Video using Google Classroom, Flipgrid, Seesaw, or a similar platform. Share these videos during an open house or back-to-school night so families can see what the students have learned.

Tips & Extensions

- For younger students, you may want to give them a set of words to start with that connect to your word study or ELA goals.

- Spelling is the obvious "gotcha" here. If using Spark Video on iPads, have students use the microphone button on their keyboard to use the "voice to text" feature. This will let them search for icons using their voice instead of having to type.

- Younger students love seeing themselves in the finished video, so you may want to encourage them to create a title slide with their picture on it and use their name in the title, for example, "Ben's Rhyming Words."

#11 Project Proposal

Students will create a proposal for a project to outline their thinking and convince someone to greenlight their future work.

Grade Level   6–12

Educational Outcomes

This project includes an introduction to the students' project or to a problem they would like to solve, research to support their thinking, and steps they will take to complete the project.

Standards Connection

Writing: presenting an argument with research

Content-area-specific standards

Time to Complete   45 minutes (with additional time for brainstorming and research)

Assistance Needed

Students will need direction regarding the type of project they will complete. The proposal could be for a project-based learning (PBL) investigation, a science experiment, a research report in a social studies classroom, or another project in which students choose their own topic.

Instructions

Before this lesson starts, students should have brainstormed and chosen a topic they would like to explore for their project.

(5 minutes)

Bring students together to state the task: "Today we are going to create a proposal for our projects. A proposal outlines the What, Why, and How of your project. It will include the steps you will take to complete the project you have chosen."

You may want to share a sample outline with your students that connects to the format or content expectations you have for this proposal:

- Title/Subtitle with picture

- Introduction to the topic (What)

- Information or research on the topic (Why)

- Steps students will take to complete the project (How)

Students should also include the following information in their proposal:

- Who will help them complete this project
- Resources for further research
- Anticipated timetable for completion

(30 minutes)
Using the format you have outlined for this assignment, send students off to create their Spark Page. You will want to circulate and provide feedback in real time.

Encourage students to use the different text options to organize their proposal. For example, the heading options can be used to create different sections. Students can also use the Quote option to share a compelling or interesting quotation related to their topic.

(10 minutes)
Have students find a partner to share their proposal with and ask for feedback. Students can share their glows (something they think is wonderful) and their grows (something to change or do differently) with their partner.

Tips & Extensions

- This project could be tailored to a business plan proposal, a request for an independent study, or any moment when students need to convince someone to approve an idea.

- Have students include the link to their Spark Page project proposal as part of their final project. They can add the link as a button on a final Spark Page that captures their entire learning journey.

#12 Sight Word Video

Practice sight word reading and help students see their own improving proficiency.

Grade Level   K–5

Educational Outcomes
Students will read sight words while recording their voice to practice fluency.

Standards Connection
Language: sight-word recognition

Time to Complete   15 minutes per day

Assistance Needed
This activity works best if using shared classroom Adobe Spark accounts, as this makes project sharing really simple. Create a video, and use the duplicate function to create a copy for each student.

Instructions

This activity requires that the teacher prepare Spark Video projects for students to use. Students then read the words in the video and record themselves doing so.

First, create a Spark Video with a single sight word per screen, and with no music or narration. You may have a set list of sight words for different groups of students in your class.

Show students how to duplicate the video and change the name of the video. They can number it to correspond with a sight word list or with a title such as Day 1. Students open the duplicated Spark Video project. Students then go through the words slide by slide, recording themselves reading them.

Over time students will have a growing collection of videos of themselves practicing the same sight words, sounding more proficient each time. Teachers and reading intervention specialists can use this video to monitor student progress.

Tips & Extensions

- Instead of using a shared classroom Adobe Spark account for this project, students can create a Video in their own account. Then students can duplicate their video each time they work with a new list of sight words.

- This activity can be used for intervention or small group instruction; for example, you could use this activity to extend a guided reading lesson.

 **TEACHER STORIES**

"My eighth-grade computer class used Spark Video to create book reports after reading *And Then There Were None* by Agatha Christie. The videos were very creative and amazingly unique from each other. My seventh-grade computer class created videos entitled: *Five Things You Don't Know about Me*. The students really enjoyed the opportunity to showcase something new to their classmates, and the website allowed them to have lots of fun while creating the videos. I really love how students can sign in through Google Drive and do not need to create new logins and passwords."

—*Yvonne Cain, technology coordinator*

#13 Digital Citizenship Spotlight

Students will share a tip for navigating a digital space or interacting online.

Grade Level   3–12

Educational Outcomes

Using their knowledge of digital citizenship and Internet safety, students will create a graphic that features an image, icon, and tip for staying safe and smart in online spaces.

Standards Connection

Writing: summarizing

Digital Citizenship: connection to current goals

Time to Complete   15 minutes (end of lesson)

Assistance Needed

This activity can be completed independently or at the conclusion of a lesson on digital citizenship. You can connect this activity to a focus area, such as searching online, commenting in online spaces, or communicating on social media.

Instructions

(5 minutes)

At the conclusion of a lesson, ask students to think about their biggest takeaway from today. Pose the question, "What tip would you give to someone to help them   [connection to topic] ?" If this is a single lesson on digital citizenship, you may want to provide a broader prompt, such as, "What is one thing someone can do to be safe online?"

Ask students to share with a partner or to jot down some of their ideas in a notebook or document. Then state today's task: "Today we are going to create graphics that provide our school community with a tip for digital citizenship. You will add text and an icon to an image to help get your message across."

Open Spark Post and show students how you add text, search for an icon, and choose a background image.

(10 minutes)

Have students use one of the tips they brainstormed to create a graphic. Encourage them to add an icon to their page that connects to the tip they shared.

If you know that your students will share their creations on a specific social media platform, or that one size is better for the type of sharing you have in mind, ask students to choose the appropriate size or resize their images.

When students are finished, have each student download their graphic as an image file. This will give you the option to use the image in class social media posts or to have students share them with their peers in a space such as Seesaw, Google Classroom, Otus, or your LMS of choice.

Tips & Extensions

- Find a local organization that is passionate about online safety and digital citizenship. Share students' Spark Post creations so they can use them on their social media platforms.

- Ask students to resize their Posts in the size of a Spark Video slide. Then combine student creations to make a movie of digital citizenship tips to share with a partner class.

 # Special Occasion Class Project

Create a fun collaborative project for special occasions, holidays, and dates commemorating events or people.

Grade Level   3–8

Educational Outcomes
Connect this project to cross-curricular learning in English Language Arts and beyond.

Standards Connection
Speaking and Listening: summarizing an event

Time to Complete   🕐 45 minutes (additional time for Teacher creation)

Assistance Needed
For this project, students create their own videos, and the teacher creates a class Spark Page. Take a picture of each student to use on the class Spark Page. The Spark Page will link to your students' individual videos.

Instructions

Student Lesson
(5 minutes)
Explain the assignment to the students, by saying something like, "Today we are going to create a video to spotlight __[special event, holiday, etc.]__." Make sure students understand that their Spark Video will be part of a classroom project with all of their videos in it. Ask students to think about the message they'd like to share in their own videos.

(15 minutes)
Ask students to create a Spark Video project. The first slide should contain their name on a title screen. Students should add three to five additional slides for their video messages. Provide guidance to students with your expectations; for example, if students are creating a video for a special occasion such as Veteran's Day or Memorial Day, offer a checklist of items students should include in their videos.

Students can use Spark Video's free public image search to find supporting imagery, or they can pull icons from Spark's huge icon library. They can then change the layout of each slide to incorporate the media they choose.

(10 minutes)

Students record a single sentence for each slide. Show them how to play back their narration, and explain that they can rerecord as needed.

(5 minutes)

After students have created their Spark Video, ask them to share the link with you.

Teacher Steps

Create a Spark Page using a classroom picture as the title background, and with the event name as the title.

Use the plus sign to add a Glideshow or a Split Layout to the Spark Page. A Glideshow will ask you to choose a background picture and add content on top of the picture, and you can add photos of your students to the Glideshow one at a time. A Split Layout allows you to have a student photo on one side of the page, and their video on the other. Both layout styles work, so pick the look that you prefer.

If you use a Glideshow, save it. Each student picture will be displayed full screen, and you'll be able to layer each student's video on top of their picture using the link the students shared with you. If using a Split Layout, add one layout for each student, with their picture on one side and their video on the other. This looks best if you alternate sides, so the first student's picture is on the left and their video is on the right; the next student's video is on the left and picture on the right, and so on,

When finished, publish the Spark Page and share the link with other teachers and family, embed it in a school newsletter, etc.

Tips & Extensions

- This project works well for events around which you want to trigger classroom discussions. Examples may be religious holidays (including Christmas and Hanukkah), commemorative dates (including Memorial Day and Martin Luther King Day), and family-oriented dates (including Mother's Day and Father's Day).

- Remember that individual student videos must be published before they can be embedded in a Spark Page.

- If using Glideshow, you'll notice that by default, Spark Videos are embedded on the left side of a Spark Page Glideshow. To make things more interesting, drag some to the center or left so that each video is placed differently (and so that you don't obscure your students' faces).

TEACHER STORIES

"My students have created Spark Videos to share memories from a special event like a field trip or special guest speaker to the school. They have also used this awesome program to put together math task video challenges by creating several pictures and adding audio or text to share the math task challenge with others. Finally, students have used Spark Video to share science experiments or STEM projects with parents by loading completed videos into their Seesaw Learning Journals."

—*Heidi Samuelson, fourth grade teacher,*
Oak Elementary School, Tennessee

#15 Perform a Poem

Students will create a Spark Video with a recording of a favorite poem or a poem they have written.

Grade Level   K–12

Educational Outcomes

Using their voice, icons, and images, students will create a movie that brings a poem to life. Students will make connections between the lines of a poem and visual content to help an audience make meaning of the words.

Standards Connection

Writing: elements of poetry

Reading Literature: poetry and fluency

Time to Complete   45 minutes

Assistance Needed

Students can use a favorite poem or a poem they have written for this project. Before starting this project, allocate time for students to either locate a poem or write their own poem.

Instructions

(10 minutes)

Share a line from a favorite class poem with your students, and pose the question, "What images or ideas come to mind when I read this line? What do you see?" Have students share with a partner.

State the task: "Today we are going to perform a poem by creating a Spark Video to bring a poem to life. You will read each line of your poem and choose an icon or image to pop up on the screen."

Model for students how to open a Spark Video project. Add a title slide, then take the line of poetry you read at the beginning of the class and record yourself saying the line of poetry. Then choose an icon or image to add to the slide. Use this time to think aloud, or discuss with students why you spoke with a certain tone in your voice or chose a particular image for the slide.

(30 minutes)

Ask students to brainstorm what type of image or icon connects to each line of the poem. Have them jot down their ideas on paper, an online document, or on a graphic organizer. After students have thought about the type of images or icons to use with each line of poetry, ask them to open a new Spark Video project.

Each slide should include a recording of one line of the poem. Students will add the image or icon to the slide and then record the line of their poem. They will continue this until they have a slide and recording for each line of poetry.

(5 minutes)
Model for students the different ways to share their project. You may want students to publish their Spark Video to a link and then share the link by posting it in Google Classroom, adding it to a Flipgrid video response, or following a different format.

Tips & Extensions

- Connect this project to a special event such as Poetry Month. Share student videos in an April newsletter.
- Have students write a poem around a theme or topic they are studying in another subject area. Use this activity as a cross-curricular connection.

#16 Multimedia Biography Reports

Students can publish biography projects that incorporate a wide variety of media. Using Spark Page, students can take a traditional biography report and curate images, videos, and online content to create a website.

Grade Level 4–12

Educational Outcomes

Students will conduct research on an individual, synthesize their findings, and create a website sharing what they have learned.

Standards Connection

Research Skills: evaluating sources
Reading Informational Text: reading to gather facts
Writing: organizing and presenting research findings

Time to Complete (45-minute lessons; research time may vary

Assistance Needed

Students may need support conducting research and evaluating sources. You may want to curate a list of high-quality websites and print materials for students to use.

Instructions

Day 1

(10 minutes)

Pose the questions to your students: "Why does someone write a biography? What is the author's purpose when writing a biography?" Ask students to think-pair-share and discuss their thoughts with a partner.

Introduce the project students will complete: "Today we are going to start a research project to learn about the life of a notable figure in history. We will use our research to create a website with Spark Page."

If you are working with a clear list of notable figures for students to learn about, such as inventors, students can pick their person to start conducting their research.

(25 minutes)

Before sending students off to begin their research, you may want to introduce an English Language Arts skill specific to your grade level. This could include using context clues to figure out the meaning of new words or noticing text structure as a reader.

As students conduct research today (and subsequent days), you may decide to circulate around the room to support students. Alternatively, you might use this time to hold one-on-one conferences to check in with each student.

(5 minutes)
Bring the class together so students can share their progress and set a goal for their research.

Day 2
After students have spent several days researching the individual they are profiling for their biography, they will be ready to write their report and publish it with Spark Page.

(10 minutes)
Bring students together to share the next step in their project. You might say, "Today we are going to share our research with the world, using Spark Page."

Introduce Spark Page to your students, showing off key features, such as how to add text, images, videos, and links to the page. For this project, you will want to show students they can create section headings, using the text feature to set a structure for their writing.

To get students started, ask them to add their title and subtitle and choose a header image. You might decide to have students follow a set format for their biography project with sections on (a) childhood, (b) accomplishments, (c) contemporaries, and more.

(25 minutes)
Students can open Spark Page and get started creating their website.

Depending on the scope of this project, you may have already had students write their biography reports in a separate document, such as Google Docs. If this is the case, students can copy and paste each paragraph into their Spark Page and add additional media such as images, videos, or links. If students are writing their biography reports for the first time, you may want to allocate more time.

(10 minutes)
Bring students together after they have finished writing their

reports. Demonstrate to students how to publish their reports so they are ready to share. In small groups, students can share their Spark Page and discuss their research process.

Tips & Extensions

- If you do not have a clear cross-curricular connection for this project, you may ask students to research a person connected to a larger theme, such as Women's History Month.
- When students publish their Spark Page, connect the link to a QR code to create an interactive display in your school.

Sp TEACHER STORIES

"This year, I was the yearbook advisor, so I had my yearbooks students use pictures we had taken throughout the year to create a variety of yearbook ads that we showed on our school's morning announcements. This allowed them to showcase the photos they took and promote our yearbook so students would know what kind of shots were going to be in the book. In addition, they created sport-specific videos to highlight the season of each sport team."

—Elyse Hernandez, yearbook teacher, Garcia-Enriquez Middle School

 # Collaborative Storytelling

Groups of students create a story together, each adding to the story in turn.

Grade Level   3–6

Educational Outcomes

Students will work together to create a narrative story that incorporates a variety of multimedia.

Standards Connection

Collaboration: students working together

Writing: narrative storytelling

Time to Complete  40 minutes

Assistance Needed

This activity tends to get loud and generates lots of giggles. Be sure to set ground rules upfront. Students should wait their turn; they can add to the story but shouldn't edit or delete other students' work, and so on.

Instructions

(5 minutes)

Organize students into small groups of four or five. Each group will share a device and create a story together.

State the task for students: "Today we are going to work together to tell a story. You will each take turns adding a sentence to a story, building upon the ideas of your classmates."

Before sending students off to create, you will want to establish a team leader, who will log into their Adobe Spark account. You also may want to share examples for students of the silly stories they can create by taking turns and working together.

(30 minutes)

Ask students to agree on a title together, or assign the first student in the group to pick the title. After the students create a title slide, they will follow the rotation outlined below.

Each student:

• Adds a slide (optionally picking a layout).

• Records the next sentence in the story.

• Adds a photo or icon to match the newly added sentence.

Plan time for each student to have two or three turns. Depending on the group you are working with, you may want to set a timer to help students move through their rotation.

(5 minutes)
When students are finished, have the group pick a theme and music to match the story. They can share their work as a link or download it to their device as a movie file.

Tips & Extensions

- For even more fun, host a screening and have each group play their video story for the class. You may want to incorporate this activity into community-building goals at the beginning of the school year or as an end-of-year celebration.
- Connect the links to each group's video to a QR code to create an interactive bulletin board full of student stories.

#18 Science Lab Reports

Students will document the steps of a science experiment, gather pictures, and reflect on their learning. They will present their process and findings in a Spark Page.

Grade Level   3–12

Educational Outcomes

After participating in a science experiment, students will share the steps they followed as they relate to the scientific method.

Standards Connection

Reading Information: conducting research on a topic

Writing: text structure and organization of material

Science: content-specific goals

Time to Complete   Steps should be tailored to science experiment/activity length

Assistance Needed

This activity is designed to connect to a science experiment your students are conducting individually, collaboratively, or as a whole group. The time allocated for the steps listed below should reflect the needs of your group and the depth of topic exploration.

Graphic Organizer

Available on page 115.

Instructions

Before the Experiment

Introduce the topic students will explore together. You might direct students to a particular guiding question, or you may have students brainstorm questions for their experiment.

At this time, you may want to share a science lab report exemplar with students. This will help them envision their final creation in Spark Page at the conclusion of their science experiment.

As students establish a guiding question, conduct research, and state a hypothesis, have them keep track of these steps in a digital space or notebook. Students will include these three sections in their lab report. During this time you can encourage students to snap pictures to document their progress.

During the Experiment

Depending on your group of students and the expectations you have for this activity, you might ask students to develop the steps for their experiment or conduct the experiment based on steps you have established.

As students complete the steps for the experiment, pause for them to snap pictures of each step and summarize their actions and observations. At the end of the experiment, students can summarize their conclusions and findings. This information will be used for their final lab report.

After the Experiment

Gather your class so students can debrief on this experience. State the task: "Today, we are going to create a lab report that shows off our science experiment. You will publish this lab report on a website to share your work."

Introduce students to Spark Page, using an interactive whiteboard or display screen. Model for students as you add a header and begin outlining your lab report. Remind students that they have already summarized the key parts of the science experiment they will include in this lab report.

As you model for students, let them see as you upload a picture and create a photo grid of images. Encourage students to create a header for each section of their lab report, using the H1 or H2 feature when adding text. You may also remind students that they can search for additional images to add to their Page or add a button for extra resources.

When students are finished constructing their lab report, have each student use the Share button to create a link to their Spark Page.

Tips & Extensions

- If your students are exploring the scientific method for the first time, you may want to share a Video from Khan Academy, BrainPOP, or TED-Ed as context.

- Find a partner class or organization to share student lab reports. You may want to schedule a Video conference with Skype, Google Hangouts, or Zoom so students can share their findings.

 TEACHER STORIES

"As the computer teacher at school, I coordinated with our sixth-grade social studies teacher to do Adobe Spark Videos related to her unit on ancient Rome. At the end of her unit, the students were allowed to pick any topic on Ancient Rome that interested them and create a presentation for the class. In the past, she had them do PowerPoints; this year, I suggested we try Adobe Spark Videos. The students made very creative videos and loved selecting their own pictures and music and doing voiceovers."

—*Melissa Sinclair, technology teacher,*
Nativity Catholic School, Virginia

#19 Public Service Announcement

Students will create a video that includes information on a topic and a clear call to action.

Grade Level   4–12

Educational Outcomes

This persuasive activity requires students to take a position, conduct research to support their argument, and present a clear call to action to their audience. Use this activity with any unit of study for cross-curricular connections.

Standards Connection

Writing: persuasive techniques

Reading Information: research and synthesizing information

Time to Complete   45 minutes (with additional time for research)

Assistance Needed

This activity asks students to present information to an audience so they will take action. You will want to gather grade-level-appropriate examples to share with students. Compile a list of ideas to help students focus on topics related to your unit of study.

Available on page 113.

Instructions

(10 minutes)

Explain to your class the purpose of a public service announcement. Pose the question, "What have you seen on television, or what videos have you seen online, where the creator of the video wanted to (1) change your mind about something, (2) provide information that could save your life, or (3) try to get you to change a behavior?"

Have students share with a partner, then engage in a whole-class discussion. Share examples of public service announcements with students. You may want to extend this portion of the lesson to engage in a discussion on the features of a public service announcement that connect to your expectations for their video.

(30 minutes—with extension)

After choosing a topic and completing research for their public service announcement, share your expectations with students. You might ask them to include any of following the specific features in their public service announcement:

- Title slide

- Clear message/position

- Compelling facts

- Icons to convey information

- Pictures related to topic

- Music to grab the attention of a viewer

- Call to action

(5 minutes)

Ask students to publish their Spark Video and share the link to their public service announcement in a collaborative space. Allow time after the lesson for students to watch their classmates' creations.

Tips & Extensions

- Reach out to a local or national organization with a mission related to the topic in your students' public service announcements. Share your students' creations with this organization, and ask them to provide feedback to students.

- Ask an expert on the topic students are exploring to participate in a video conference with your students. Before students create their videos, have them ask questions to the expert to help refine their angle for their call to action.

#20 Digital Bulletin Boards

Students can show off their creations of any shape and size through pictures and summaries shared on a class Spark Page. This teacher-created page can include snapshots of student work traditionally featured on a bulletin board so that they can be shared digitally.

Grade Level   K–12

Educational Outcomes
A digital bulletin board can extend the audience for any type of student work.

Standards Connection
Writing: summarizing

Specific content area goals of original activity

Time to Complete   10-minute student writing activity. Time varies for teacher creation

Assistance Needed
This activity combines digital and analog. You or your students will want to snap a picture of classwork, write a summary, and compile these media into a Spark Page.

Instructions

Student Writing
The digital bulletin board for your class will include an explanation of the student activity, photographs of their work, and a caption written by students. Allocate a few minutes of a lesson for students to write a caption for their photo. You might share examples or a handful of sentence starters:

- In this picture you can see…
- During this project I learned…
- I chose to create a…

You could ask older students to write a one- or two-sentence summary of their work and share this with you in Google Classroom or as an email. This will allow you to copy and paste their text responses into Spark Page. Alternatively, you may ask students to tell you their caption verbally as you add it to a Spark Page.

Student/Teacher Prep
This digital bulletin board will combine photos of student work with captions. You will want to have all of the photos of student work saved to the same device you will use to create your Spark Page. Another option

is to save all images to an account in Dropbox or another service that is easily accessible in Spark. You may snap all of these pictures yourself, or ask students to snap a picture of their work and send this to you along with the caption they created.

Teacher Creation

To create a digital bulletin board, open a new Spark Page. At the top of the Page, add a title, subtitle, and a picture for the background. In the first section, use the text option to add an overview of the project you are featuring on this page. For example, if this Spark Page will showcase student dioramas on the life cycle of frogs, explain this in a few sentences at the top of the page.

Use the photos option to upload each student photo. After you add each student photo, you can copy and paste the caption they sent you. If you do not have captions for the pictures of student work, you might decide to use the photo grid option and upload the photos similarly to a collage.

Throughout the Spark Page you create, you have the option to add other features related to the student project. For example, you may want to embed a video connected to the topic students studied or search for additional pictures to add to the page.

Once you are finished adding student work to your Spark Page, use the Share button at the top of the screen to create a shareable link. Now your student work is off of a traditional bulletin board and in a digital space, ready to share with the world.

Tips & Extensions

- Students can use a voice-recording tool such as Vocaroo to record a summary of their project. They can share this link so it can be added to the Spark Page as a button.

- Before removing a bulletin board of student work, use this strategy to create a long-lasting, digital celebration of student work. Turn the link to this digital bulletin board into a QR code and make an "archives" section of your bulletin board so visitors can see student work from earlier in the school year.

TEACHER STORIES

"I teach EFL at Portuguese state schools from primary-aged students up to secondary level. My 10th graders are very keen on using Adobe Spark Video as narrated portfolios. Lately, they have developed a special interest in using Adobe Spark Post to come up with short wrap-ups of content learnt during class or as attention-grabbers for ideas."

—Carla Ferreira, EFL teacher,
Third-Cycle and Secondary Portuguese Schools

#21 ABC Movies

Students will use vocabulary words on a new topic. Using Spark Video, students will create a class movie to share new vocabulary related to a topic.

Grade Level   K–2

Educational Outcomes

Students will explore new vocabulary words and describe each word using voice and visuals.

Standards Connection

Speaking and Listening: clearly explaining vocabulary

Reading: exploring new vocabulary in context

Writing: creating sentences to describe vocabulary words

Time to Complete   🕐 45 minutes

Assistance Needed

Students may need support with identifying keywords when searching for icons. You may want to model how to search for icons using a few different keywords.

Available on page 116.

Instructions

(10 minutes)

Introduce your students to a set of vocabulary words. You might display the words on an interactive whiteboard or project each word. As you point to each word and remind students of its meaning, ask them to turn and talk to a partner as they say a sentence with each word. If you are studying communities with your first-grade students, for example, you might ask students to turn to a partner and use the word *neighborhood* in a sentence.

Although you may want to have a word starting with each letter of the alphabet for your ABC Movie, you may decide to simply select ten to fifteen words related to a topic and organize them in alphabetical order.

(25 minutes)

State the task for today's lesson: "Today we are going to create a class movie where we share important words related to __[topic]__ . You will each be in charge of one word. You will decide how to explain that word and what picture will pop up on the screen as you talk."

Model for students how a picture can act as a symbol that represents each word. For example, if you share the word neighborhood with your class, a picture of a tree or a building can represent this word.

Distribute a word to each student along with paper for them to write or illustrate. Ask students to draw a picture that represents their word. If your students can write sentences, they can use space on the page for this as well.

To create this collaborative movie, first log in to your Spark account. Open Spark Video and create a title slide for your class movie. As students begin to draw an illustration for each word, call them over one by one. Students do not need to be finished and can jump in and out of their drawings as they take turns recording the audio.

When students come to you, ask them to tell you what they will say to share their word. After students practice, they can record their voice on their Spark Video slide. Students can then give you a keyword to search for an icon. Using the search tool, let students pick the icon to pop up on the screen as their voice plays.

Repeat this process with each student. If you want to rearrange the student recordings in alphabetical order, you can move the Spark Video slides into a different order.

(10 minutes)

After all students have recorded their voice and chosen an icon, bring your students back together. You might ask the whole class, "What type of music should play in our video? What type of music connects to the theme/tone we want our audience to feel?"

Play the movie for the class so they can hear and see the final product and celebrate the work of their peers.

Tips & Extensions

- Although this activity is designed for a collaborative K–2 classroom, it can be tailored to different grade levels for independent or group work.

- A microphone attached to your device can cut down on background noise in your classroom as students record their voice.

 **TEACHER STORIES**

"Students at our high school created a variety of projects using Adobe Spark Post. Students in the Literature classes create their own book promos to build interest in a book they wanted to share with other students. One of our Spanish classes created collages about their childhood."

—*Claudio Zavala, Jr., instructional technology coordinator, Duncanville ISD, Texas*

#22 Document a Field Trip

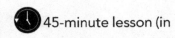

Students will capture images and create a narrative to reflect on their learning after a field trip

Grade Level   2–12

Educational Outcomes
After taking part in a field trip, students can describe what they've learned through a multimedia product.

Standards Connection
Speaking and Listening: capturing mood and tone

Reading Information: collecting facts and details about a place

Writing: composing a narrative

Time to Complete   45-minute lesson (in addition to field trip)

Assistance Needed
Students may need reminders during a field trip to capture media strategically. You will want to offer support that is tailored to the specific needs of your group.

Available on page 117.

Instructions

Before the Field Trip
Gather students before a field trip takes place to introduce them to the technology tools they will use to capture media during their field trip. Older students might each use a personal device; younger students might share a tablet with chaperone monitors.

State the task for their creation: "Today you will capture images and important facts while on our field trip. Tomorrow you will create a movie that documents the field trip, using Spark Video. As you take part in the field trip today, snap pictures or jot down notes you would like to include in your video."

After the Field Trip
(5 minutes)
Gather students to debrief after the field trip. You might pose questions such as, "What was one thing that surprised you?" or "What should everyone know about this place?"

Place students in pairs or small groups and ask them to talk about their favorite moments from the field trip. Restate the task for today: "Today you will use the images you captured from the field trip to create a short movie that shares what you learned from our field trip."

(35 minutes)

Introduce students to Spark Video, and share the key features of the tool. You will want to show students how to record their voice, add text, and upload images. Model for students as you quickly create one or two slides. If you have a checklist or graphic organizers for students to use, you can distribute them before the students dive in.

Then, ask one team leader to log into Spark Video. The groups of students will work together to create their movie. As you circulate, support students who may want to add additional media such as icons or video.

As you observe students creating their video, you may want to pause and ask for everyone's attention as you show additional features during their independent work time. For example, after students have worked with their partner for 10 minutes, you might pause the group and show them how to move text around their screen or duplicate a slide.

(5 minutes)

Bring the class back together and combine two pairs or small groups of students. Have each group share their video with one another. They can ask for feedback or share something they loved about their partner group's creation.

Tips & Extensions

- To ensure that students have an adequate set of trip images to use, you may want to take pictures of your own and put them in a shared classroom folder (perhaps on Google Drive or Dropbox) and encourage students to use these in addition to their own.

- Supplemental materials such as a checklist or storyboard can help students as they plan for their video.

- An audience for a field trip video could include a tour guide to say thank you, organization that might welcome a promotional video, partner class to share learning.

- This activity can be tailored toward a particular English Language Arts goal such as using descriptive language or creating a hook for an audience.

 TEACHER STORIES

"I exposed my students to many tech tools that would help them show what they know. A student used Adobe Spark to create a book trailer. This was his vehicle of choice, and it was so successful that I used it as an example when I presented the outcome to the Board of Education."

—*Patricia Emerson,*
eighth grade language arts teacher

#23 Captioning a Special School Moment

Students will capture a special moment from a school event and create a shareable graphic that includes a quotation, summary, or keyword description.

Grade Level   3–12

Educational Outcomes
Keeping their audience in mind, students will create a social graphic to communicate an idea to a reader.

Standards Connection
Writing: describing an event

Time to Complete   25-minute lesson
(additional time for capturing pictures)

Assistance Needed
This activity asks students to take pictures, choose a picture, and create a Spark Post with text. You may need to allocate time for students to capture pictures during an event or build this into an established activity. Students can create a Spark Post on any device; however, you will want to make sure that students can access the pictures they took on this same device.

Instructions

Instructions

(5 minutes)
Ask students to open their device and look through the pictures they took from a special school event. Encourage students to review these pictures with a classmate, side by side. As students talk about the pictures they captured, ask them to narrow down to their top three images.

(5 minutes)
State the task for today's lesson: "Today we are going to take the photographs you captured during __[school event]__. You will choose text to add to the image to make sure it is ready for sharing our special event with the world!"

Model for students as you add text to an image using Spark Post. You may want to follow a set format with your class or use a sentence starter. Here are a few options:

Before the event, ask students to interview a few people and jot down a quotation.

After the event, ask students to write a sentence documenting their favorite moment or a big takeaway.

After the event, ask students to jot down three to five adjectives to describe how they felt.

(10 minutes)
Have students open Spark Post on their device. You may want to review certain features or ask them to create a post with school colors, or in a particular size. Students can use any or all of their top three images as the background for their Spark Post.

(5 minutes)
After students have created their Spark Post, ask them to share it with you. They might save it as a link or download it as an image file. Then students can share their Spark Post using Google Classroom, Seesaw, or a similar platform.

Tips & Extensions

- Before a school event takes place, discuss with students what types of pictures they want to capture. This will help them stay on the lookout for special moments.

- Partner with a community organization looking for content to share on their social media platforms. For example, a local newspaper may want to share student-captured moments on their Instagram account.

#24 Creating Engaging Slides for Presentations

Students can use Spark Post to create slides for a presentation to communicate and share content with visuals.

Grade Level   4–12

Educational Outcomes

After conducting research and creating a presentation on a topic, students can use Spark Post to create engaging slide designs.

Standards Connection

Speaking and Listening: creating visual aids

Writing: communicating theme with colors and imagery

Time to Complete   45-minute lesson

Assistance Needed

Students should have a complete presentation before jumping into this activity. In addition to allocating class time for this task, you may want to give students the option to complete this outside of class hours.

Available on page 118.

Instructions

(5 minutes)

Display a presentation to students that includes text and a plain background. If you have created a project exemplar for students, remove images and set to a simple font and color scheme.

Pose the questions, "If I want my audience to understand this concept, what images should I include? If I want my audience to feel a certain way when I give my presentation, what color scheme or font should I include?" Ask students to share their answers with a neighbor and then engage students in a whole class discussion.

(5 minutes)

State the task for today's lesson: "Today you will create slides that help your audience connect with the topic you are sharing in your presentation. You will choose a background, color scheme, and visuals to help communicate your vision."

Introduce students to Spark Post. Show them how you can choose a size for your slide and alter the background with solid colors or images. Model for students how to add text to Spark Post to create a title slide and update presentation slides.

(30 minutes)

Ask students to open their presentation and Spark Post on their device. They might toggle from one web browser or app to another, or split their screen to view both at the same time. Before students get started, you may want them to jot down a few ideas they have for images, icons, color scheme, and font.

Encourage students to start by creating a title slide and then move through their slide deck to create additional slides. As students work, you may want to show them extra tips such as how to duplicate a slide. Use mid-lesson interruptions to quickly bring your class together for a 30-second demo of a new feature you didn't initially introduce.

The way students save their slide design will depend on the device they use. When students save their slide design as a JPEG (picture file), they can add it to their slide deck as a background image. Students using Google Slides, PowerPoint, or Keynote will use the same steps to Insert an image. Encourage students to add their new slide design to their presentation as they create each new slide.

(5 minutes)

At the end of the lesson, ask students to form groups of three. In these small groups, students can share one or two of their slide designs and ask for feedback from their peers. Students can continue finishing their slides after class or during time allocated the next day.

Tips & Extensions

- Instruct students to choose Widescreen or Standard Spark Post sizes that correspond to their slide deck.

- If your students have access to the Premium Spark features, you might encourage them to use the colors they have added to their personal brand across all slides.

- Here are a few extra tips for teachers and students using Spark Post and Google Slides: http://bit.ly/SlidesandPost

#25 Classroom Newsletter

A teacher-created classroom newsletter can spotlight student work and share information with families and the school community.

Grade Level   K–12

Educational Outcomes

A classroom newsletter can be a vehicle for giving student work an audience outside of your classroom. Students can contribute to a monthly newsletter created by their teacher.

Standards Connection

Subject-area-specific standards related to classwork

Time to Complete   30–45 minutes (time will vary)

Assistance Needed

This activity can include a variety of student-created content. Before creating your Classroom Newsletter, ask students to submit ideas of what you should include, or to suggest one recent piece of their work to include in the newsletter.

Instructions

A classroom newsletter can include a variety of components. Before opening up a new Spark Page project, decide what information you would like to include in a monthly newsletter for families.

Your newsletter could include any of the following:

- A recap of events from the previous month
- Pictures of students at work
- Links to student work
- Embedded YouTube videos with information on a topic students will study
- Links to resources for families (e.g., Google Form for volunteer sign-ups, district calendar with important dates)

Teacher Steps

Open Spark Page and choose a title and subtitle. Upload a picture for the background or search for a thematic image. Use the plus sign below the header to add content to your page. You will want to use the H1 and H2 header buttons to organize the information into categories.

As you add information to the page, don't forget the Button feature. This lets you add a link to any website. The Video feature lets you embed videos. This is perfect for adding student work created with

Spark Video. If you have many student pictures to share, you might decide to use the Photo Grid feature to create a collage of photos with one caption.

Optional Student Role

Students can take on the role of reporters and work individually or in pairs to create content for a school newsletter. You could have one student in your class write a one-paragraph summary of a field trip and another student write a paragraph about a special visitor who came to your school. Students can write their content for the classroom newsletter and share it with you as an email or post in an LMS. Copy and paste their text into your Spark Page.

Tips & Extensions

- You might create a new Spark Page for each month and have a unique link to each classroom newsletter. If you have used Spark Page to create a class website, you can link these two pages by using the Button feature on your class website.

- Ask each student to pose holding a favorite book they've read this past month, displaying a project they finished, or showing something they are proud of accomplishing. Use these photos in your classroom newsletter.

#26 Spot Math in Action

Students will explore their classroom and spaces in their community to capture pictures of math in action. They will create a Spark Post with a picture and caption describing the mathematical moments all around them.

Grade Level   K–12

Educational Outcomes

To place relevancy on the math concepts they explore in the classroom, students will locate examples of math principles during the school day.

Standards Connection

Math: connection to content-specific learning goal

Writing: crafting a label and caption

Time to Complete   45 minutes

Assistance Needed

This lesson should connect to the specific math topic your students are learning. You will want to model examples that connect to your learning goals.

Available on page 119.

Instructions

(10 minutes)

Start today's lesson by posing the question, "Where do you see math outside of the classroom?" You might tailor this opening question to connect to topics your students are studying, such as shapes, formulas, or another unit of study. Give students a few minutes to discuss with a partner and circulate to listen in on their conversations.

Bring students together and share some of the things you heard students talk about. On an interactive whiteboard or projection screen, show students three to five pictures that demonstrate a math topic you are learning in a real-world space. For example, if you are studying types of triangles with your class, share a few pictures of scalene triangles in a space such as the school library.

(10 minutes)

State the task for today's lesson: "Today you will take pictures that show off __[our math topic]__ in action. You will work with a partner to take pictures, and then we will add captions and labels to our pictures."

Have students work with a partner to snap pictures of "math in action." You might ask students to search in the classroom or explore different spaces in the school building. If students are not familiar with how to use the camera on their device, take a moment to remind students how to snap pictures.

(20 minutes)
Bring students back together and open Spark Post on your device. Show students how to choose a size for their graphic and upload one of their pictures. You will also want to model how to add text to the screen. Depending on the expectations you have for students, you will want to model how you write a sentence describing how the picture shows math in action.

Students can work in pairs or independently to create a handful of Spark Post graphics that show math in action around the classroom or school building. You may want students to create images with particular dimensions if you plan on sharing them in a specific space. For example, if you plan on sharing student-created Spark Posts on a class Instagram page, students can create graphics in the shape of a square.

(5 minutes)
Have students share their Spark Post images in an online space such as Google Classroom or Seesaw. Students can view each other's designs and leave feedback.

Tips & Extensions

- After students have submitted their Spark Post creations, add each one to a slide in Google Slides so students have a shared document with all of their findings.

- Use the images students have created for a bulletin board display.

- Turn the images into augmented reality triggers using Aurasma. Connect each image to content hosted online, such as Spark Video math tutorials students have created on a similar topic.

#27 Publish Google Docs

Provide a way for students to share their work with the world by publishing their writing (Google Doc) on a website (Spark Page).

Grade Level   3–12

Educational Outcomes

After completing a writing assignment, students will combine their text with multimedia to create a website that showcases their work.

Standards Connection

Writing: publishing

Writing: curating digital media

Time to Complete   45-minute lesson
(after writing activity)

Assistance Needed

Students will need to have completed a writing assignment in Google Docs. This writing could include a science lab report, research paper, persuasive essay, or any type of writing assignment students are ready to publish.

Instructions

(10 minutes)

After students have completed a writing assignment in Google Docs, bring the class together to publish their work with Spark Page. State the task for today's lesson: "Today you will take the writing you have finished in Google Docs and publish it with Spark Page. You will choose images that connect to your topic and choose a theme to communicate your message clearly to your audience."

Open Spark Page in a separate window (or as a separate app). Add a title, subtitle, and background image to the page. Let students listen as you think aloud and search or choose a picture for your header image.

Model for students as you open your exemplar Google Doc on the screen. Resolve any lingering comments or track changes. Copy the entire text of the document. In Spark Page, choose the option to add text. Paste the entire text from your Google Doc into the text box. You will automatically see (+) signs to add additional media in between each paragraph.

Pose the questions to the class, "What type of images should I add to my Spark Page to help my reader make sense of my writing? What type of images will you add to your Page?" Ask students to share their thoughts with a partner.

(25 minutes)

Have students open a Google Doc and Spark Page on their device. They will follow the same steps you modeled to add the text of their writing to their Spark Page. As students search for pictures to add to their page, encourage them to use a variety of keywords. You may want to brainstorm these search terms with the whole class or provide time for students to jot down keywords before creating their Spark Page.

As students work on transforming their writing to a shareable Spark Page, pause to remind them to choose a theme for their creation. You may want to discuss how font, colors, and text structure can influence the way someone perceives their writing. For example, if the topic is of a serious nature, such as endangered species, they may want to avoid choosing a font that is too playful or whimsical.

(10 minutes)

Show students how to share their work by creating a link. Model for students as you post the link in a shared space. This could include an LMS such as Schoology, Otus, or Google Classroom.

During this time, students can share their work with a partner or head over to a shared online space where their peers have posted their work.

Tips & Extensions

- Establish a relevant, authentic audience at the start of a lesson. If students are publishing their lab reports with Spark Page, for example, you may want to share the links with a professor at a local university who can provide feedback on their work.

- Make connections to digital citizenship initiatives when students are providing feedback on the work of their classmates.

#28 Curiosity Wall

Before starting a new unit of study, students can create graphics that spotlight the questions they have about a new topic. These student explorations can help drive the focus of a new unit of study.

Grade Level   2–12

Educational Outcomes
Students will share what they want to know about a topic by writing questions.

Standards Connection
Writing: crafting questions

Time to Complete   25 minutes (plus introduction/extension)

Assistance Needed
This activity is designed to kick off a new unit of study or exploration into a topic. You can also tailor this activity as an extension to a previously discussed topic you would like to explore further with students.

Instructions

(5 minutes)
Gather students together and introduce them to the new topic of study. If your students are about to learn about natural disasters in a science class, for example, show a slideshow of pictures or play a short BrainPOP video.

Pose these questions to your class: "What do you wonder about this topic? What questions do you have? What would you like to know more about this topic?" Ask students to share with a partner as you listen in to their conversations.

You might list a few questions students have on chart paper or an interactive whiteboard or share some of your own wonderings about the topic.

(15 minutes)
State the task for today's lesson: "Today you will capture your wonderings and share them with your classmates on a Wonder Wall. You will use Spark Post to create graphics that combine your questions with images."

Take a quick moment to show students how to log in to Spark Post, choose a picture, and add text to their creation. Remind students that they can create more than one Spark Post, and to download each one to their computer or publish each one as a link.

As students work to create their question cards, remind them to make the text large enough for someone to read from far away. You will also want to encourage students to choose an image for the background that connects to their question.

(5 minutes)

Bring students together and show them how to share their Spark Post. If you will share their creations on a bulletin board for a Wonder Wall, ask students to download their Spark Post as a picture file. Give students a moment to share one of their questions with a partner. They can turn their screens toward one another and share their Spark Post creations.

Tips & Extensions

- Use the graphics students create with Spark Post for a bulletin board full of student wonderings. If students make their graphics in the shape of a square, you can display the Spark Post creations like a quilt.

- Ask students to form a small group and choose one wondering they have. Give students time to create game plan for finding answers or more information about the question their classmate posed.

- The questions student pose can help drive future instruction. It gives you a window into student interest and can help you decide on the direction and focus of lessons in an upcoming unit.

#29 Destination Wish

Students will create a video that spotlights a place they would like to visit. This activity can be tailored to specific content area or English Language Arts learning goals.

Grade Level   K–12

Educational Outcomes
Students will share details about a place they would like to visit, using a variety of sources to gather information.

Standards Connection
Writing: synthesizing information from multiple sources

Reading Information: reading to gather information

Time to Complete   (2) 45-minute lessons (may allocate additional research time)

Assistance Needed
K–2 students may need additional support adding their voice to each slide and searching for images and icons. You might decide to have students conduct research on different places and create a collaborative video instead of individual movies.

Graphic Organizer

Available on page 121.

Instructions

Day 1
(5 minutes)
Pose the question to your class, "What is a place you would like to visit? If you could go anywhere in the world, where would you go?" Ask students to share with a partner. If you are tailoring this project to a specific area of the world, add this to your questions.

(5 minutes)
State the task for today's lesson: "Today we are going to gather information about a place we would like to visit. We will use this information to create a video all about this special destination."

Model for students as you search for information on a place you would like to visit. Collect information on a Google Doc, or in a notebook, graphic organizer, or other location that is similar to how students will keep track of their notes.

(30 minutes)

Send students off to locate information on the destination they wish to visit. If you are connecting this project to particular learning goals, such as using descriptive language or conducting an interview to gather information, you will want to introduce these expectations to students before they begin research.

Depending on the support your students need, you might send them off right away to search independently or curate research materials for students that are both print and digital.

(5 minutes)

Ask students to review their notes from today and choose one fact about the place they want to visit that they think is interesting. Have students share this information with a partner.

If you would like students to complete additional research, extend the research portion of this activity another day or ask students to come to class tomorrow with more information for their video.

Day 2
(5 minutes)

Gather the class to review your goal for today: "Today we will take the research we conducted and share the facts we learned in a Spark Video. You will want to introduce your destination, share facts you learned through your research, and provide a closing message that tells your audience why this place is important."

If students are using Spark Video for the first time, take a moment to show how to start a video project by adding a title and adding content to a slide. Younger students may need additional support as they record their voice to share what they learned.

(30 minutes)

Share your expectations for this project and state what should be included, such as a title slide, introduction to the destination, interesting facts, and closing statement. Students can jot down their ideas before starting their video if you would like them to plan a script.

Send students off to create their Spark Video while you circulate around the classroom. If you anticipate that certain students will need additional support with searching for images or icons related to a location, consider forming a small group to support these students.

(10 minutes)
Provide time for students to share their work to a link or to download their movie as a video file. If you are sharing student Spark Video creations in a particular space, you will want to direct students to create a link or share a file.

In pairs or small groups, have students share their Spark Videos to their peers. You may want students to record a question they have about their classmate's video on a sticky note or as a post in a discussion forum.

Tips & Extensions

- Create a single Spark Page to feature all of the student videos. You can embed each Spark Video creation on your class Spark Page or use the Button tool to link to each student's video.
- Have each student turn the link to their Spark Video into a QR code, using a tool such as QRstuff.com. Create a bulletin board with a map and ask each student to add the QR code to their Video to the corresponding location.

#30 Showcase a Discovery

Students will conduct research on a topic and showcase a fact, concept, or idea they "discovered" through their search. This project can include a synthesis of information from various sources. Students will showcase their discovery in a video with a combination of media.

Grade Level   3–12

Educational Outcomes

After researching a topic, students will pinpoint one idea worth sharing. They will create a script based on their research and locate images and icons to help tell the story of their learning.

Standards Connection

Informational Writing: composing a script

Informational Reading: conducting research

Content-area-specific goals

Time to Complete   45-minute lesson
(additional time for research)

Assistance Needed

This activity can be tailored to any content area. You will want to determine the expectations for the final student product before introducing this activity to students. If you are asking students to conduct research from multiple sources, you may want to curate the reading materials.

Available on page 122.

Instructions

Before Video Creation

State the task for this activity: "Today we are going to start conducting research on ___[topic]___. Our goal is to create a Spark Video that showcases a discovery you made. This could include an interesting fact, information that surprised you, or something you think everyone should know about."

At this time, you may want to share a video exemplar with students to help them envision the final product.

Direct students to research materials you have curated, or allow students to navigate online spaces or a school library to gather information on their topic. You may want to provide a graphic organizer to help students as they conduct their research.

(5 minutes)

Provide time for students to review their research. Ask them to identify two "discoveries" from their research they would like to share with the world. Encourage students to share their two ideas with a classmate, then decide on which one they would like to use for their "discovery video."

(5 minutes)

Remind students of the task for this activity. You may want to replay any project exemplars you have shared or share a rubric outlining specific expectations.

Here is a sample breakdown of the slides students can organize for their video:

1: Title Slide with teaser
2: Why this topic is interesting/exciting/surprising
3–5: Facts about topic
6: Where to go to get more information
7: Closing statement

(25 minutes)

Open Spark Video to model for the class how to get started with a video project. You may want to allocate more time for this step if students are brand new to the tool. As students dive into Spark Video, you may want to pause and share tips about choosing a theme connected to their message and selecting music related to the topic.

Provide time for students to create their video. You may want to extend this time frame, depending on the depth of your students' research.

(10 minutes)

Have students form small groups of three to four students. Allow each student to play their video for their group. Ask students to provide a Glow (something they loved) and a grow (something to improve on) for each video they watch.

Tips & Extensions

- Student Discovery videos can be used to kick off a new unit of study. One option is to provide a list of topics for students to explore that connect to the learning goals outlined in this new unit.

- Instead of connecting this activity to a specific content area, you may want to give students the option to choose from a wide range of topics. This is perfect for moments when you are focusing on ELA skills, such as sequencing events or reading for research.

 **TEACHER STORIES**

"I have used Adobe Spark in my health classes as a getting-to-know-you, icebreaker activity. It's a great way to introduce students to each other by sharing adventures or interests."

—*Beckie Stevenson,*
Crystal Lake South High School, Illinois

#31 Share a Research Question

Students will decide on a research question and create a Spark Post to share their research question and an image related to their topic. Students will also brainstorm hashtags that could be used if their design is shared on social media.

Grade Level   3–12

Educational Outcomes

Once students have decided on a topic for a project, they will create a question to guide their research. As students get ready to gather information on this topic, they will create a list of related topics.

Standards Connection

Informational Writing: composing a research question

Informational Writing: using domain-specific vocabulary

Content-area-specific goals

Time to Complete   30 minutes

Assistance Needed

This activity can be tailored to any subject area. As students prepare research questions, you may want them to follow a specific format. To spark student curiosity, curate videos for students to explore related to the topic.

Instructions

Before Creating Questions

Before asking students to write research questions, provide time for them to learn about different aspects of the topic you are studying. The amount of time you carve out for this activity will depend on the amount of background knowledge your students will need before writing research questions.

If your class is studying the circulatory system of the body, for example, direct students to a YouTube playlist with TED-Ed videos that cover a range of subtopics in this area. Provide time inside or outside of the classroom for students to watch videos or read articles that will spark their curiosity.

(10 minutes)

State the task for today's lesson: "Today we are going to write research questions for our project on ___[topic]___. You will write a question to research that relates to what we have explored so far."

Provide examples of research questions:
- How are blood types different?
- How does your body heal when you get a paper cut?
- What causes someone's heart rate to change?

Ask students to jot down a few questions they have and share their questions with a partner. Provide time for students to solicit and give feedback before deciding on one question.

(15 minutes)
Introduce Spark Post to students. Model how to search for a picture related to your topic and add a research question as text. Let students watch as you think aloud about what font, colors, and style connects to your topic. As students use Spark Post to create a graphic, circulate and support as needed.

(5 minutes)
After students have created their research question graphic, provide time for sharing. Have students turn to a partner and share, or post their graphic in a discussion thread and include a sentence describing why they chose their question, or both!

Tips & Extensions

- Students can incorporate the Spark Post they create into a research report made with Spark Video or Page. They can use this as a title slide or introductory image.
- Collect all student research questions to create a slideshow to kick off an open house for families. You could also print out these Spark Post designs and post them on a bulletin board.

#32 Giving Eyes to the Exit Slip

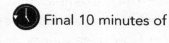

Students will reflect on what they learned during a lesson. Using Spark Post, students will create an exit slip that is ready to share publicly on social media or class social spaces.

Grade Level   3–12

Educational Outcomes

Students will reflect on their learning in a concise manner and provide formative assessment data.

Standards Connection

Writing: publishing for an authentic audience

Content-area-specific learning goals

Time to Complete   Final 10 minutes of any lesson

Assistance Needed

Students may need support searching for images or navigating the design options in Spark Post during their first time using the tool.

Graphic Organizer

Available on page 123.

Instructions

This activity is designed to be added to the end of an existing lesson. To check for understanding through an exit slip, you can provide a prompt for students related to your specific learning goal.

If your students are learning about the Women's Suffrage Movement, tell them to "Choose one moment from the Women's Suffrage Movement that was crucial for helping women receive the right to vote. Support your position in one sentence."

Alternatively, if your students are studying rocks and minerals, you might say, "What is one way that rocks and minerals are different from one another?"

(Step 1)

State the closing activity for today's lesson: "Today you will create a Spark Post to share what you learned about __[topic/learning goal]__."

Pose the question you would like students to answer, and ask them to take a moment to share their ideas with a partner.

(Step 2)

Open Spark Post and model for students how to create a digital exit slip. Use the text tool to show students how to add their answer/response to their Spark Post. Ask each student to compose their answer and type it into their Spark Post exit slip. Students can also use the text tool to add their name to their Spark Post.

(Step 3)
Demonstrate to students how to add a picture to the background of their exit slip. Let them watch as you think aloud and choose a keyword to use as a search term. Depending on the subject area you are teaching, you may want to brainstorm keywords with students to help them find a picture connected to your topic.

(Step 4)
Provide time for students to customize the design of their exit slip, including changing the font, colors, and style of their Spark Post.

(Step 5)
Decide on how you would like students to share their Spark Posts. You may want students to download their exit slip as a picture file or publish their exit slip with a link. Model this step for students by choosing either option.

Ask students to finish their Spark Post and share their exit slip. If you want to their peers to see their Spark Post, have them submit their exit slip in Google Classroom. If you have permission to share student work on social media, choose a handful of exit slips to post on a class Twitter feed or Instagram page.

Tips & Extensions

- If you know that you will share student exit slips on a particular social media platform, instruct all students to choose the appropriate shape for their design.

- Students can use the resize tool in Spark Post to change the dimensions of their design at any time.

- Instead of giving all students the same prompt, differentiate the question for your class.

#33 Curate Research Materials

Researching and evaluating resources is an important skill for students. Using Spark Page, students can create an annotated bibliography of research material on a topic.

Grade Level   3–12

Educational Outcomes

Students will create a website with links to research materials and an explanation of each resource.

Standards Connection

Reading Informational Text: gathering information

Reading Informational Text: evaluating sources

Writing: summarizing main idea

Time to Complete   (2) 45-minute lessons

Assistance Needed

Students may need support navigating search engines as they look for resources on their topic. You may want to model how to use keywords to search for information on a site such as Google.

Available on page 124.

Instructions

Day 1

(10 minutes)

State your goal for students: "Today we are going to look at online sources and decide whether they are a good place to gather information on a topic."

Pose the following questions: "When you visit a website, how do you know whether the information is accurate? How can you be sure that a website is high quality?" Ask students to think-pair-share and discuss their ideas.

Bring the class together and share examples of high-quality websites related to your content area. For example, if your students will study endangered species this year, you may want to show off special features of National Geographic's website.

(30 minutes)

State the task for today's lesson: "Today you will search for websites that include information on your topic. You will decide whether they are high quality and worth sharing with other people interested in learning more about your topic."

Before sending students off to search for websites, model how you can bookmark a website by either adding the link to online notes (e.g., Google Doc) or jotting down the information in a notebook or graphic organizer. Show students how you add a few sentences in your notes on why you think this website is worth sharing.

Students can work independently or with peers to search for websites related to their topic. Remind students to jot down a reason for why a particular website contains useful information on their topic.

Depending on the task you have defined for students, you may want to specify a target number of resources for them to collect.

(5 minutes)

In small groups or as a whole class, ask students to share what they noticed as researchers today. You might ask the question, "What are some things you came across today that surprised you about the quality of different websites?"

Day 2

(10 minutes)

State the task for today's lesson: "Today you will use your research from yesterday to create a Spark Page with links to your curated resources. You will include a link to the websites you found yesterday and an explanation of why this website is worth exploring."

Open Spark Page and show students how to add a title and subtitle to their page. Using the text tool, show students how to add a few sentences that explain why a website is worth someone else visiting.

Then show students how to use the button tool to add a link to the website you have just described.

(30 minutes)
Explain to students that they will repeat the steps you modeled to create a website full of their favorite resources on a topic. You can also encourage them to add additional images to their page related to their topic.

(5 minutes)
Show students how to publish their Spark Page by using the Share button on their screen. Ask students to post the link to their Spark Page in a shared space for their peers to view. This could include a shared Google Doc, a Seesaw post, or a post in a discussion thread in the LMS your school is using.

Tips & Extensions

- This lesson can connect to a digital citizenship initiative at your school. Tailor the expectations to align with these goals.
- Ask students to create a Spark Video on their topic, sharing five interesting facts they learned. Students can embed the Spark Video on their Spark Page.

#34 Foreign Language Vocabulary Practice

Students can practice using new vocabulary words in a foreign language classroom. Using Spark Video, students can create a slideshow that spotlights new vocabulary words and records their voice as icons appear on the screen.

Grade Level   6–12

Educational Outcomes

Students will use new vocabulary words to create sentences, demonstrating how the new words are used in conversation.

Standards Connection

Speaking and Listening: creating a presentation

Language Arts: using new vocabulary words

Writing: composing sentences

Time to Complete   45 minutes

Assistance Needed

Students may need support with identifying keywords when searching for icons. You may want to model how to search for icons using a few different keywords.

Instructions

(5 minutes)

Distribute a list of new vocabulary words to your students. Introduce each word to the students. Pose the question, "When would you use this new set of words?" or "Can you try using one of these words in a sentence?" Ask students to share their answer at their tables or with a classmate.

State the task for today's lesson: "Today you will write sentences using our new vocabulary words and create a slideshow to combine icons with your sentences."

(10 minutes)

Using the words on the vocabulary list, ask students to create five to ten sentences. Each sentence should contain one of the new vocabulary words. As students compose their sentences, circulate to provide support and allow students to bounce ideas off their peers.

Ask students to brainstorm a visual to accompany each sentence. For example, students may be learning transportation vocabulary in the Spanish-language classroom, and their featured word is *arrival*. They can jot down several search terms (plane landing, train station) that will help them find an icon to match their sentence.

(20 minutes)

Introduce Spark Video to students, pointing out key features such as how to add text to a slide and how to search for icons. You might say, "Locate one icon for each slide that connects with your sentence. Record your voice as you say the sentence on the matching slide."

Students can work independently to create their Spark Video, but before sending them off to work, remind them to include a title slide, to introduce themselves on a slide, and any other expectations you have for their creation. Also ask them to choose a theme and music for their Video.

(10 minutes)

When students have finished their videos, have them find a partner. Each student can share their video, and offer glows (something they liked) and Grows (advice on something they can improve).

Within this time, students can brainstorm an audience for their videos beyond their classmates. This could include a partner class studying the same topic or native speakers who can provide feedback on their creation.

Tips & Extensions

- Have students add their videos to a shared folder or post in a discussion forum so they can use these creations to review vocabulary.

- You may want to introduce these words to students before class and ask them to arrive with sentences they have created.

- Students can work in pairs for this activity, taking turns recording their voice and working together to craft sentences and search for icons.

 # #35 Explore Keyword Searches

Students will use domain-specific vocabulary to locate images and icons. Using brainstorming, sketching, and conversations, students will determine keywords for media searches.

Grade Level K–12

Educational Outcomes

With this lesson, students will take a deep dive into vocabulary connected to any unit of study.

Standards Connection

Reading: making meaning of new words

Language Arts: apply domain-specific vocabulary in different contexts

Content-area-specific goals of original activity

Time to Complete 45 minutes

Assistance Needed

This activity asks students to brainstorm a list of keywords to use as search terms. It can be tailored to any type of activity using the Spark tools. You will want to model for students and customize the lesson for your subject area and content-specific goals. This lesson might be used as an "add on."

Available on page 125.

Instructions

(10 minutes)

Bring students together in front of a chart paper or interactive display screen. Pose the question, "If I want to find pictures of ___[topic]___, what type of search terms could I use?" Ask students to work with a partner to come up with five to seven keywords. After students have discussed with a peer, compile a list as a class.

Open the Spark tool you will use with your class. If you are practicing locating search terms as a one-day activity, you may want to use Spark Post. Alternatively, if your students are already completing an activity in Spark Video or Page, use that tool.

Model for students as you think aloud and search for images or icons. For example, if you are searching for pictures for a project exemplar on the American Revolution, let students hear you think aloud as you type in search terms until you find an image or icon you would like to use.

(10 minutes)

State the task for today's lesson: "Today we are going to search for __[images/icons]__ related to our topic. You will add the media you find to your __[Spark Post/Page/Video]__ ."

Before students open the Spark tool they are using for this activity, ask them to brainstorm a list of keywords to use as search terms. You might ask them to work collaboratively with a partner or small group exploring the same topic. Students can use a graphic organizer, notebook, or digital space to collect their ideas.

(20 minutes)

Ask students to open the Spark tool and use the search terms to find the perfect images or icons for their project. Encourage students to try multiple keywords before deciding on one type of media.

As you circulate and support students, encourage them to think of a word someone else might use to describe the same idea or object. Depending on the device your students are using, you may encourage them to use the voice-to-text tool on their keyboard to enter search terms that might be hard for them to spell.

(5 minutes)

To wrap up this lesson, have students share with a partner some of the obstacles and successes they had when searching for images. Encourage students to share ways they were able to find an image or icon when it was difficult at first.

Tips & Extensions

- When students prepare to search for images, encourage them to think about the tone or mood they want to communicate to their audience. You may want to show examples of bright and colorful images to students, or pictures that are of a darker color scheme.

- Connect this lesson to digital citizenship goals around safe searches. You may want to use this activity as an extension for a digital citizenship lesson.

#36 Sequence Short Stories

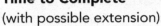

Students will retell a short story they have read or tell a story from their own life. Using Spark Video, students will practice telling stories in sequence in just five to ten sentences.

Grade Level   K–12

Educational Outcomes

By retelling a story, students will use temporal words to demonstrate understanding of sequence and order of events.

Standards Connection

Speaking and Listening: telling a story to an audience

Reading Literature: retelling stories or using stories as exemplars

Writing: sharing a story in narrative format

Time to Complete   🕐 45-minute lesson
(with possible extension)

Assistance Needed

Students may need support putting the events of a story in order. You may want to spend time brainstorming story ideas before the lesson if students are telling their own story. Alternatively, you may want to read aloud or share a story for students to read if they will retell a story.

Graphic Organizer

Available on page 126.

Instructions

(5 minutes)

State the task for today's lesson: "Today you will tell a short story from your own life (or retell a story we've read). You will put the story in order using words such as first, then, next, and finally; tell the story in just a few sentences. After we practice telling our stories to a classmate, you will create a Spark Video sharing your story."

Introduce the term temporal words to students. Temporal words signal the passage of time. You may want to display a list of words you expect students to use. These words may connect to your English Language Arts standards.

Model for students your own telling of a story; you may want to use a graphic organizer to have students write their short story. This writing exercise might include just five short sentences, or it can be extended to connect to a longer writing activity.

(10 minutes)

Have students choose a moment from their own lives (or a story they have read). On paper or a digital space, give students time to tell a story in just a few sentences. Remind them to use temporal words such as first, then, next, and finally. If you would like to extend this writing activity, you might devote an entire class period to brainstorming and writing.

(25 minutes)

Bring students together to model movie making with Spark Video. Show students how you open Spark Video on your device and add a title to your story. Encourage students to record each sentence to a different slide. After students have recorded their voice, they can search for images and icons that connect to each sentence.

As students work to publish their writing, pause them periodically to remind them how to change the theme of their video to fit their story. You also may want to model for students as you "think aloud" when choosing music for your model. For example, as students watch you decide on which music to play in the background, you might think aloud, "My story is very serious, so I want to choose music that feels the same way. This type of music would be a good fit."

(5 minutes)

Students will save their video as a movie file or create a link to share their movie. In pairs, ask students to share their video with a partner. Students can post their video link or upload their video file in a classroom learning management system such as Google Classroom, Seesaw, or Schoology.

Tips & Extensions

- This type of activity can be used as a reading response for students. Ask students to choose five important moments to summarize what took place in their book and create a Spark Video that shares each event in sequence.

- If students are writing personal narratives, they can publish their writing on Spark Page.

- A Spark Video created with this type of activity could include highlights from their personal narrative. Students can embed their Spark Video on their Spark Page.

#37 Virtual School Tour

Show off the work happening at your school by creating videos that take virtual visitors around the building. Students can take community members and families on a tour of their school.

Grade Level   K–12

Educational Outcomes

With a focus on summarizing important information, students will create a video that uses media they have captured and curated. The angle of the student videos may include persuasive writing elements and a call to action for viewers.

Standards Connection

Narrative Writing: providing detailed descriptions

Persuasive Writing: presenting a call to action

Time to Complete   45-minute lesson (additional time needed to collect images and video)

Assistance Needed

This activity can be scaled to different grade levels. You may want younger students to provide ideas of places to spotlight on a school tour. You may want older students to create their own school tour videos in groups of two or three.

Graphic Organizer

Available on page 127.

Instructions

Before Video Creation

Ask students to create a list of important places in their school building. You might pose the question, "Which spots in the school would you show off to a new student or a visitor?" Using this list, as a whole class or in small groups, ask students to snap pictures of these places.

If you would like students to interview members of the school community, you might also pose the question, "Who are some of the important people in our school building?" Students can use the camera on their device to record a short interview with school staff members such as the school nurse or custodian.

(10 minutes)

State the task for today's lesson: "Today we are going to create a video to help someone take a virtual tour of our school building. You will use the photos and videos you gathered to create a school-tour video."

School tour videos can follow a set format. You will want to tailor expectations to connect with content area goals such as conducting an interview or summarizing information. Share this information with students when you introduce this activity. Here is a sample outline for a school tour video:

1: Title Slide with school picture
2: Location
3–7: Spotlight of special places in the school building
8–9: Interviews with spotlight staff members
10: Call to action (e.g., visit our school)

Introduce students to Spark Video. Make sure to point out certain features such as the cropping tool in the video upload option, or how to search for icons. If students have captured their own video and photographs, you'll want them to access this media on the device they are using to create their Spark Video.

(30 minutes)

Provide time for students to create their video. You may want to allocate time for students to plan, using a graphic organizer, or to write a script for their videos. As students work on their Spark Video, pause them periodically to provide tips related to theme and music selection. You may want to encourage students to use a microphone or find a quiet place in the classroom to record their narration.

(5 minutes)

If students worked in groups to create their school tour video, combine two groups. In these larger groups, students can share their two videos and ask for feedback. Depending on your norms around peer feedback in your classroom, you may want to allocate additional time for students to make changes to their video before publishing.

Tips & Extensions

- With the video feature in Spark, you can have students capture special moments to add to a school tour video. You might ask students to capture video on a tablet and share it to a teacher device or team leader device.

- Use the video students create as promotional material to share on a school website or social media channels. With the branding feature in Spark, it's easy to tailor the color scheme to match your school's logo.

#38 Digital Portfolios

Students will show off their learning from the school year. They will present their success stories, accomplishments and struggles in a Spark Page.

Grade Level   3–12

Educational Outcomes

Students will collect work samples across a variety of subject areas to chronicle their learning.

Standards Connection

Writing: summarizing

Writing: publishing for an audience

Time to Complete   Initial 25 minutes, with periodically scheduled updates at the end of a unit/culminating project)

Assistance Needed

Students should have a selection of work they would like to feature. This could include photographs of projects, links to work published online, or videos.

Instructions

Creating a Portfolio

(5 minutes)

Pose the questions to students, "What have you accomplished so far this year that you are proud of? Why is a digital portfolio useful for students to have?"

State the task for the lesson: "Today we are going to set up a digital portfolio. Over the course of the school year we will carve out time to add pieces of work we are proud of and want to share with others."

Open Spark Page and model for students as you add your name as a title and "Digital Portfolio [school year]" as the subtitle. Let students watch as you search for a picture for the header that connects to the school year. Show students how they can use the text feature to add a heading and description of each piece of work they add to their portfolio. You will also want to model how students can link to other work they have created, using the button tool or video tool to embed video.

(15 minutes)

Send students off to create their digital portfolio. They may only have one or two things to add at this time. Students can focus on adding pictures of their work, linking content from other places and providing a description of each project or activity they have featured.

As students are working on their digital portfolios, you can circulate to encourage them to add more details, choose a theme, or set up headings for future projects that they will spotlight.

Adding to a Portfolio

Over the course of the school year, pause periodically to provide an opportunity for students to add new artifacts to their digital portfolio. You may want students to add new pieces of work in chronological order or give students more flexibility with the way they organize their work.

As students add to their portfolio, they can use the Share button to update the link to their Spark Page. When students add work to their digital portfolio over the course of the school year, the link will update every time they hit the Share button.

Tips & Extensions

- Once students publish their Spark Page, there are lots of ways they can share their digital portfolio with the world. One way they can share their work is by connecting the link to their digital portfolio to a QR code.

- Spark Page is perfect for simple portfolios, especially when working with younger students. More sophisticated students, especially those engaged in media and arts classes, may want to consider using Adobe Portfolio instead (This is a paid service and is included in Adobe Creative Cloud for EDU deployments).

#39 Goal Setting

Students can capture their goals for the school year, a new unit of study, or the very next day, using a combination of Spark tools. Customizing this experience gives students choice on sharing their goals.

Grade Level   K–12

Educational Outcomes

Using a combination of media, students will write or record their goals and choose an image(s) to connect to their idea.

Standards Connection

Writing: composing sentences

Content-area-specific goals of original activity

Time to Complete   30-minute lesson with time varying based on project scale

Assistance Needed

This activity asks students to establish a goal and share it through a Post, Page, or Video. You may want to have individual goal setting conversations with students, share student data to help form goals, or provide content-area-specific examples of goals.

Instructions

(10 minutes)

Gather students together and pose the question, "What would you like to accomplish ___[this year/week/unit]___?" Remind students to be specific as you give them time to share with a partner.

Share a few examples of goals that are attainable and measurable. Depending on the group of students you are working with, you may want to use specific vocabulary that will resonate with them. Ask students to decide on one goal to capture today.

(15 minutes—with potential extension)

Decide whether your students will use Spark Post, Page, or Video to capture their goal.

Spark Post: perfect for a quick activity and if you'd like students to create a class slideshow of goals or share goals on social media

Spark Page: perfect for a text-rich response in which students will outline the steps to accomplish their goal and update their page with their progress

Spark Video: perfect for using voice to capture goals and to share a clear sequence of action items they will take to reach their goal

State the task for today's lesson: "Today we are going to create a __[Post/Page/Video]__ to capture our goal related to __[topic]__." Add any specific information related to the expectations you have for this activity.

Quickly introduce the Spark tool you would like students to use for this activity and send them off to capture their goal. As you circulate and support students, you may want to pause the class as they work independently and share an additional tip or strategy.

(5 minutes)

Ask students to share their work with a partner or small group. You might decide to showcase every student's Spark Post on a class Instagram page or have students post a link to their Spark Page or Video in a class LMS for their peers to view.

Tips & Extensions

- Connect this goal-setting activity to conversations with families and students around progress. Share these creations with families during virtual and on-site meetings.

- If students use Spark Post to create their goals, ask them to choose the Square size. Once they download the image file, you can create a slideshow with each student's Post, using Spark Video to add the student's voice to their image.

#40 Reflection Collection

Students can collect their reflections on accomplishments, successes, and obstacles over the course of the school year on a personalized website.

Grade Level   3–12

Educational Outcomes

By pausing periodically over the course of the school year, students can reflect on their learning and chronicle their growth.

Standards Connection

Writing: summarizing

Writing: publishing for an audience

Time to Complete   15 minutes (once a month or periodically throughout the school year)

Assistance Needed

Students may need support with the initial setup of their Spark Page. You may need to remind students to publish their Page after making updates.

Available on page 120.

Instructions

Set Up

(5 minutes)

State the task for today's lesson: "Today you will set up a website we will update periodically over the school year. This space is for capturing reflections on our learning, including accomplishments, success stories, and obstacles."

Pose the question, "What is something that has felt successful in our class this year? What has felt like an obstacle?" Ask students to share their answers at their tables or with a classmate.

(10 minutes)

Introduce students to Spark Page. Model for students how to open Spark Page and how to choose a title, subtitle, and a header image for the page. You may want to have students follow a specific model, or you may want to give students more flexibility.

For example, for each entry, students might set the date as an H1 or H2 heading. Then they can add their reflection in paragraph format beneath the heading. You may want to show students how you add both the date and a short reflection to your own Page.

After students have set up their Page, ask them to add an introduction that shares the purpose of their Reflection Collection. You may want students to discuss how reflecting on their growth during the school year can help them make plans and set goals for the future.

(5 minutes)

Show students how to share their Page by creating a link. You may want them to post this link in a shared space such as Google Classroom or another LMS. Remind students that each time they update their Page with a new reflection they must share the page again to update the link.

Periodically

(15 minutes)

Once a month, or more frequently throughout the school year, carve out time for students to write a short reflection to add to their Reflection Collection page. You might provide a prompt for students that relates to a specific topic or event.

Students can add their new reflection to the Spark Page they set up earlier in the school year. You might ask students to add images, videos, or links to something they created during this time period or to a resource they reference in their reflection.

After students have made their new entry, ask them to use the Share button to update their link. These Reflection Collection pages can become part of a student portfolio at the end of the school year. They can also be used to facilitate goal setting conversations during one-on-one conferences.

Tips & Extensions

- Students can type their reflections in another document (e.g., Google Docs, Microsoft Word) and copy and paste it into their Spark Page.

- Encourage students to capture images over the course of the school year. They can add these to their Reflection Collection.

- Ask students to share their Reflection Collection with a mentor or advisor as they make updates during the school year.

A note to readers . . .

These graphic organizers are designed to support your students as they dive into the projects outlined in this book.

You may want to use these graphic organizers on days when students have limited access to technology and to prepare for tech-rich learning experiences with Spark.

You can access these graphic organizers as a Google Doc template using this link: bit.ly/SparkOrganizers.

Public Service Announcement

Video Book Report

Science Lab Report

ABC Movies

Document a Field Trip

Creating Engaging Slides for Presentations

Spot Math in Action

Reflection Collection

Destination Wish

Showcase a Discovery

Giving Eyes to the Exit Slip

Curate Research Materials

Explore Keyword Searches

Sequence Short Stories

Virtual School Tour

Public Service Announcement

Name _____

Topic _____

Call to Action
What do you want someone to do after they watch your video?

_____

_____

Research
What compelling information can you share to change someone's mind on this subject?

_____

_____

Images
What photos should flash across the screen to grab someone's attention?

_____

_____

Icons
What symbols connect to your topic/message?

_____

_____

Music
How do you want someone to feel when they watch your video?

_____

_____

Theme
What colors/emotions connect to your topic?

_____

_____

Video Book Report

Name _____

Book Title _____

Author _____

Genre _____

Five-Sentence Summary
What is this book about?

_____

_____

_____

Characters
Who are the main characters in this book?
What makes them special?

_____

_____

_____

Setting
Where does this story take place?

_____

_____

_____

Recommendation
Would you encourage a friend to read this book? Why or why not?

_____

_____

Science Lab Report

Name _____

Topic/Title_____

Guiding Question
What will you investigate in this experiment?

_____

_____

Research
What have you learned about this topic?

_____

_____

Hypothesis
What do you think will happen during your experiment? What is your educated guess for the conclusion?

_____

_____

_____

Steps
What steps did you follow? What would someone else have to do to replicate your experiment?

_____

_____

Conclusion
What did you figure out based on your experiment? What would you do differently next time?

_____

_____

_____

ABC Movies

Name _____

Topic _____

My Letter_____

My Word_____

What kind of picture or icon will I need?

_____

_____

_____

_____

_____

What will I say about my word?

_____

_____

_____

_____

_____

_____

Document a Field Trip

Name _____

Field Trip Destination _____

Slides

	What will you see on the screen?	What will you say?
Title Slide		
Where did you go?		
Why did you go there?		
Fact #1		
Fact #2		
Fact #3		
Why should someone else visit this place?		

Creating Engaging Slides for Presentations

Name _____

Presentation Title _____

Presentation Summary
What is your presentation about?
_____
_____

Audience
Who is going to see your presentation?
_____
_____

Response
How do you want your audience to feel during your presentation?
_____
_____

Action
*What would you like someone to do after viewing
your presentation?*
_____
_____

Colors
*What colors connect to the content or mood of your presentation?
(e.g., bright, dark)*
_____
_____

Font
*What type of font do you want to use in your presentation? (e.g.,
serious, playful)*
_____
_____

Visuals
What images and icons will you include in your presentation?
_____
_____

Spot Math in Action

Name _____

Before
What are you looking for?

_____

_____

_____

_____

Where will you look?

_____

_____

_____

After
What did you find?

_____

_____

_____

What captions or labels will you include on your picture?

_____

_____

_____

_____

Reflection Collection

Name _____

Date _____

What have you accomplished during this month/unit?

_____

_____

_____

_____

_____

What has felt successful during this time?

_____

_____

_____

_____

What obstacles have you encountered/overcome during this time?

_____

_____

_____

_____

_____

Destination Wish

Name _____

Place
Where would you like to visit?

_____

_____

_____

Location
Where is this place? What important details should someone know about its location?

_____

_____

_____

Significance
What makes this place special? Why do you want to visit this place?

_____

_____

_____

Closing
What will you say on your last few slides to make sure your audience knows this place is important to you?

_____

_____

_____

Showcase a Discovery

Name _____

Topic_____

Title_____

Slides

Slide #	What will appear on your slide?	What will you say? narration/script

Giving Eyes to the Exit Slip

Name _____

My response to the question/prompt

_____

_____

_____

_____

_____

_____

Keywords I can use to search for images

_____

_____

_____

_____

_____

Colors related to my topic

_____

_____

_____

_____

_____

Curate Research Materials

Name _____

Research Topic_____

Resource #1
Description

_____

_____

_____

Link

_____

Resource #2
Description

_____

_____

_____

Link

_____

Resource #3
Description

_____

_____

_____

Link

_____

Explore Keyword Searches

Name _____

Topic _____

What kind of image do I want to include? (e.g., a picture of mountains on a foggy day)	*What keywords can I use as search terms?* (e.g., mountain, foggy, landscape, daytime)

Sequence Short Stories

Name _____

Title _____

First,
Sentence

_____

Visual

_____

Then,
Sentence

_____

Visual

_____

Next,
Sentence

_____

Visual

_____

Next,
Sentence

_____

Visual

_____

Finally,
Sentence

_____

Visual

_____

Virtual School Tour

Name _____

Topic_____

Call to Action_____

Slides

Slide #	What will appear on your slide?	What will you say? narration/script

Spark Creativity at Your School!

Let's stay connected!

Host an "Injecting Creativity into Your Classroom with Adobe Spark" Workshop at Your School

―――――――

Visit Adobe Education Exchange:
https://edex.adobe.com/en/spark

―――――――

Schedule the Authors for a Keynote Presentation

―――――――

For more information or to request a workshop, contact . . .

Dr. Monica Burns

info@classtechtips.com

 @classtechtips

 @classtechtips

Ben Forta

ben@forta.com

http://forta.com

 @benforta

More Books from EdTechTeam Press
edtechteam.com/books

The HyperDoc Handbook
Digital Lesson Design Using Google Apps
By Lisa Highfill, Kelly Hilton, and Sarah Landis

The HyperDoc Handbook is a practical reference guide for all K–12 educators who want to transform their teaching into blended-learning environments. *The HyperDoc Handbook* is a bestselling book that strikes the perfect balance between pedagogy and how-to tips while also providing ready-to-use lesson plans to get you started with HyperDocs right away.

Innovate with iPad
Lessons to Transform Learning
By Karen Lirenman and Kristen Wideen

Written by two primary teachers, this book provides a complete selection of clearly explained, engaging, open-ended lessons to change the way you use iPad with students at home or in the classroom. It features downloadable task cards, student-created examples, and extension ideas to use with your students. Whether you have access to one iPad for your entire class or one for each student, these lessons will help you transform learning in your classroom.

The Space
A Guide for Educators
By Rebecca Louise Hare and Robert Dillon

The Space supports the conversation around revolution happening in education today concerning the reshaping of school spaces. This book goes well beyond the ideas for learning-space design that focuses on Pinterest-perfect classrooms and instead discusses real and practical ways to design learning spaces that support and drive learning.

Classroom Management in the Digital Age
Effective Practices for Technology-Rich Learning Spaces
  By Patrick Green and Heather Dowd

Classroom Management in the Digital Age helps guide and support teachers through the new landscape of device-rich classrooms. It provides practical strategies to novice and expert educators alike who want to maximize learning and minimize distraction. Learn how to keep up with the times while limiting time wasters and senseless screen-staring time.

The Google Apps Guidebook
Lessons, Activities, and Projects Created by Students for Teachers
  By Kern Kelley and the Tech Sherpas

The Google Apps Guidebook is filled with great ideas for the classroom from the voice of the students themselves. Each chapter introduces an engaging project that teaches students (and teachers) how to use one of Google's powerful tools. Projects are differentiated for a variety of age ranges and can be adapted for most content areas.

Code in Every Class
How All Educators Can Teach Programming
  By Kevin Brookhouser and Ria Megnin

In *Code in Every Class*, Kevin Brookhouser and Ria Megnin explain why computer science is critical to your students' future success. With lesson ideas and step-by-step instruction, they show you how to take tech education into your own hands and open a world of opportunities to your students. And here's the best news: You don't have to be a computer genius to teach the basics of coding.

Making Your School Something Special
Enhance Learning, Build Confidence, and Foster Success at Every Level
   By Rushton Hurley

In *Making Your School Something Special*, educator and international speaker Rushton Hurley explores the mindsets, activities, and technology that make for great learning. You'll learn how to create strong learning activities and make your school a place where students and teachers alike want to be—because it's where they feel energized, inspired and special.

Making Your Teaching Something Special
50 Simple Ways to Become a Better Teacher
   By Rushton Hurley

In the second book in his series, Rushton Hurley highlights key areas of teaching that play a part in shaping your success as an educator. Whether you are finding your way as a brand new teacher or are a seasoned teacher who is looking for some powerful ideas, this book offers inspiration and practical advice to help you make this year your best yet.

The Google Cardboard Book
Explore, Engage, and Educate with Virtual Reality
   An EdTechTeam Collaboration

In *The Google Cardboard Book*, EdTechTeam trainers and leaders offer step-by-step instructions on how to use virtual reality technology in your classroom—no matter what subject you teach. You'll learn what tools you need (and how affordable they can be), which apps to start with, and how to view, capture, and share 360° videos and images.

Transforming Libraries
A Toolkit for Innovators, Makers, and Seekers
 By Ron Starker

In the Digital Age, it's more important than ever for libraries to evolve into gathering points for collaboration, spaces for innovation, and places where authentic learning occurs. In *Transforming Libraries*, Ron Starker reveals ways to make libraries makerspaces, innovation centers, community commons, and learning design studios that engage multiple forms of intelligence.

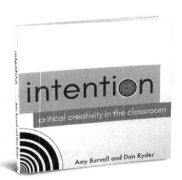

Intention
Critical Creativity in the Classroom
 By Amy Burvall and Dan Ryder

Inspiring and exploring creativity opens pathways for students to use creative expression to demonstrate content knowledge, critical thinking, and the problem solving that will serve them best no matter what their futures may bring. Intention offers a collection of ideas, activities, and reasons for bringing creativity to every lesson.

The Conference Companion
Sketchnotes, Doodles, and Creative Play for Teaching and Learning
 By Becky Green

Wherever you are learning, whatever your doodle comfort level, this jovial notebook is your buddy. Sketchnotes, doodles, and creative play await both you and your students. Part workshop, part journal, and part sketchbook, these simple and light-hearted scaffolds and lessons will transform your listening and learning experiences while providing creative inspiration for your classroom.

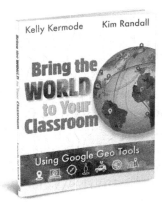

Bring the World to Your Classroom
Using Google Geo Tools
  By Kelly Kermode and Kim Randall

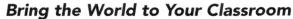

We live and work in a global society, but many students have only a very small community or neighborhood as their frame of reference. Expand their horizons and help them increase their understanding of how they fit in the global landscape using Google Geo Tools. This book is packed full of how-tos and sample projects to get you and your learners moving forward with mapping, exploring, and making connections to the world around you.

50 Ways to Use YouTube in the Classroom
  By Patrick Green

Your students are already accessing YouTube, so why not meet them where they are as consumers of information? By using the tools they choose, you can maximize their understanding in ways that matter. *50 Ways to Use YouTube in the Classroom* is an accessible guide that will improve your teaching, your students' learning, and your classroom culture.

Illuminate
Technology Enhanced Learning
  By Bethany Petty

In *Illuminate*, author, educator, and technology trainer Bethany Petty explains how to use technology to improve your students' learning experiences. You'll learn specific how-tos for using a wide variety of apps and tools as well as the why behind using technology. Meet your students' needs and make learning memorable using technology enhanced learning.

The Martians in Your Classroom
STEM in Every Learning Space
   By Rachael Mann and Stephen Sandford

In *The Martians in Your Classroom*, educator Rachael Mann and former Director of Space Technology Exploration at NASA Stephen Sandford reveal the urgent need for science, technology, engineering, and math (STEM) and career and technical education (CTE) in every learning space. Proposing an international endeavor to stimulate students' interest in science and technology, they highlight the important roles educators, business leaders, and politicians can play in advancing STEM in schools.

More Now
A Message from the Future for the Educators of Today
   By Mark Wagner, PhD

The priorities and processes of education must change if we are going to prepare students for their future. In *More Now*, EdTechTeam Founder Mark Wagner, explores the six essential elements of effective school change: courageous leaders, empowered teachers, student agency, inspiring spaces, robust infrastructure, and engaged communities. You'll learn from educational leaders, teachers, and technologists how you can make each of these essential elements part of your school or district culture—starting now.

The Top 50 Chrome Extensions for the Classroom
   By Christopher Craft, PhD

If you've ever wished there were a way to add more minutes to the day, Chrome Extensions just may be the answer. In *The Top 50 Chrome Extensions for the Classroom*, you'll learn time-saving tips and efficiency tricks that will help reduce the amount of time spent in lesson preparation and administrative tasks—so you can spend more time with students.

Sign up to learn more about new and upcoming books at
bit.ly/edtechteambooks

About the Authors

Ben Forta is Adobe Inc.'s senior director of Education Initiatives, where he spends his time teaching, talking, and writing about Adobe products, creativity, and digital literacy, and providing feedback to help shape the future direction of Adobe products. Ben is the author of more than forty books with more than 750,000 copies in print in English and titles translated into fifteen languages. Many of these titles are used as textbooks in colleges and universities worldwide. Education is Ben's passion. Between writing, lecturing, and in-classroom experience, Ben has dedicated his professional and personal lives to teaching, inspiring, and sharing his love for technology and creativity. He is immensely grateful to have had the opportunity to share with millions worldwide. Ben is a successful entrepreneur with experience creating, building, and selling start-ups. He is a sought-after public speaker, a writer and blogger, and he lectures and presents on education and development topics worldwide.

Connect with Ben

forta.com

twitter.com/benforta

Dr. Monica Burns is a curriculum and educational technology consultant, Apple Distinguished Educator, and founder of ClassTechTips.com. As a classroom teacher, Monica used one-to-one technology to create engaging, standards-based lessons for students. Monica has presented to teachers, administrators, and tech enthusiasts at numerous national and international conferences including SXSWedu, ISTE, FETC, and EduTECH. Monica is the author of several books including *Tasks Before Apps: Designing Rigorous Learning in a Tech-Rich Classroom*. Monica visits schools across the country to work with PreK–20 teachers to make technology integration meaningful and purposeful. You can find out more about working with Monica, and her books and resources by visiting ClassTechTips.com.

Connect with Monica

Twitter.com/classtechtips

Facebook.com/classtechtips

Pinterest.com/classtechtips

Instagram.com/classtechtips

Made in the USA
Middletown, DE
01 September 2019